Keith
Enjoyed meeting you
Live Ready

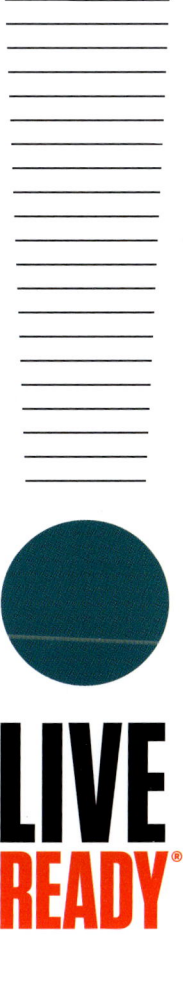

DEDICATION

To you, the reader, for having the courage to start your journey to Live Ready!

ADVANCE PRAISE FOR
LIVE READY®—BEYOND THINK AND GROW RICH.

I am delighted to say that this book supports the *Think and Grow Rich* principles by Napoleon Hill in every way, with an up-to-date style, in the voice of David R. Ibarra.

—**DON GREEN**,
EXECUTIVE DIRECTOR AND CEO
OF THE NAPOLEON HILL FOUNDATION

This is not a book. It is an invitation to profound growth. Ibarra will challenge you to greater self-honesty, persuade you of a better way of doing life, then patiently mentor you to turn breakthrough ideas into potent habits. Use it as prescribed and you will be rewarded forever.

—**JOSEPH GRENNY**,
NEW YORK TIMES BESTSELLING AUTHOR OF
CRUCIAL CONVERSATIONS AND *CRUCIAL INFLUENCE*

Are you ready to dream big, find your purpose, and fuel your burning desire? David will share how you can conceive, believe and achieve your Life Purpose.

—**SHARON LECHTER**,
AUTHOR OF *THINK AND GROW RICH FOR WOMEN*
AND CO-AUTHOR OF *NEW YORK TIMES* BESTSELLER
RICH DAD POOR DAD

Live Ready — Beyond Think and Grow Rich is the ultimate guide to bringing your dreams into reality. David Ibarra's delivery of the critical elements needed to construct a Rhythm of Success, told through real-world stories of individuals who live these principles, makes for a compelling call to action.

—**TRACEY C. JONES, PH.D.**,
AUTHOR OF EIGHT BOOKS AND PRESIDENT,
TREMENDOUS LEADERSHIP

DAVID R. IBARRA

LIVE.
READY

BEYOND
Think and Grow Rich

LIVE READY® – BEYOND Think and Grow Rich.
Copyright © 2023 by David R. Ibarra
All rights reserved. Printed in the U.S.A.

Tremendous Leadership
PO Box 267 • Boiling Springs, PA, 17007
(717) 701 - 8159 • (800) 233 - 2665
www.TremendousLeadership.com

Tremendous Leadership's titles may be bulk purchased for business or promotional use or for special sales. Please contact Tremendous Leadership for more information.

Tremendous Leadership and its logo are trademarks of Tremendous Leadership. All rights reserved.

No part of this publication may be reproduced, stored in or introduced into a retrieval system, or transmitted in any form, or by any means (electronic, mechanical, photocopying, recording, or otherwise) without prior written permission of both the copyright owner and the above publisher of this book except by a newspaper or magazine reviewer who wishes to quote brief passages in connection with a review.

Requests for permission to reproduce material from this work should be sent to:
Permissions
eLeaderTech Incorporated
Ibarra Business Centre
438 East 200 South
Salt Lake City, Utah 84111

∞ The paper used in this book meets the minimum requirements of ANSI/NISO Z39.48-1992 (R1997) (Permanence of Paper).

ISBN 978-1-961202-07-8 (hardcover)
ISBN 978-1-961202-06-1 (paperback)
ISBN 978-1-961202-08-5 (e-book)

BOOK AND COVER DESIGN: EmDash, Austin
DESIGNED & PRINTED IN THE UNITED STATES OF AMERICA

TABLE OF CONTENTS

INTRODUCTION *by David R. Ibarra*	8
INTRODUCTION *by Don Green*	11
FOREWORD *by Sharon Lechter*	12
CHAPTER ONE *The Power of Thought*	15
CHAPTER TWO *The Power of Purpose*	41
CHAPTER THREE *Specialized Talent Team*	63
CHAPTER FOUR *Faith-Based Action*	79
CHAPTER FIVE *Readiness Mindset*	95
CHAPTER SIX *Pleasing Personality*	113
CHAPTER SEVEN *Adversity Adjustment*	129
CHAPTER EIGHT *Sound Health*	143
CHAPTER NINE *Optimizing Time and Money*	163
CHAPTER TEN *The Promise*	181
IN GRATITUDE & ACKNOWLEDGEMENT	187
MEET DAVID R. IBARRA	189

INTRODUCTION

by David R. Ibarra

As a disciple of *Think and Grow Rich* and the *Science of Success Philosophy* by Napoleon Hill, my life purpose is to work primarily with employed adults who get up every Monday morning and go to jobs they really do not enjoy. These adults are quietly suffocating in unhappiness because they live in a negative fear-based thought setting.

I'm passionate about helping these adults because I understand what it feels like. Like many of you, my life has been a winding road rather than a straight path toward success. My journey started with most of the first 14 years of my childhood in foster care, wondering if I mattered. I became a very angry young man and a poor student, who often found himself in trouble. I was struggling to make it through each day, each month, and each year. I often wondered if success was meant for me.

Then everything changed! At just 18-years old, I had no idea my dishwasher job at a Farrell's Ice Cream Parlour Restaurant would turn out to be one of the most significant experiences of my life. I met Mr. Robert E. Farrell, who became my first business coach and mentor. Mr. Farrell challenged me to study *Think & Grow Rich* by Dr. Napoleon Hill and become a disciple of its Principles of Success.

Mr. Farrell helped me dream big, find my purpose, gain a burning desire, believe it, and then achieve it. I learned how to become the *Switch Master of My Own Thought* and pivot to a *Positive* joy-based thought setting. As I promised Mr. Farrell, I became a disciple of Dr. Napoleon Hill's principles. I learned how to apply them to create a productive, profitable, happy life, and then, to pay Mr. Farrell's kindness forward I began teaching others to do the same.

Think and Grow Rich, along with Mr. Farrell's mentorship, changed my life forever—and it allowed me to help many others conquer work so they could become better partners, better parents, better neighbors, and better members of their communities. Over the course of my career, I have shared Dr. Hill's *Science of Success Philosophy* with thousands of people seeking to achieve their goals, objectives, or *Life Purpose.*

As a disciple of Napoleon Hill's success principles, I've taken it upon myself to ensure that the principles he taught remain relevant and applicable in modern society. Therefore, I present to you my new book, *Live Ready® – Beyond Think and Grow Rich.*

INTRODUCTION

by Don Green

As the Executive Director of *The Napoleon Hill Foundation* and a fellow disciple of Dr. Napoleon Hills' work, I understand the responsibility of sharing his ideas with as many people as possible. Dr. Hill challenged disciples of his work to teach his Principles of Success in their own words, with the aim of helping people improve themselves and get what they could and should have in life.

David R. Ibarra has done just that. His newest book, *Live Ready® – Beyond Think and Grow Rich,* teaches the *Science of Success* principles in a modern story telling way.

I was privileged to be able to collaborate with David to ensure that this book upholds the *Think and Grow Rich* principles discovered by Dr. Napoleon Hill. I am delighted to say that this book supports the original philosophy in every way, with an up-to-date style in the voice of David R. Ibarra. *Live Ready®–Beyond Think and Grow Rich* is compassionate, considerate, comprehensive, and easy to understand. I believe you will enjoy this book as much as I did.

FOREWORD

by Sharon Lechter

A TRUSTED MENTOR GAVE DAVID IBARRA A COPY OF *Think and Grow Rich* at an early age and it shaped the trajectory of the rest of his life. He now shares Hill's wisdom and teachings with those seeking and ready to create abundance in their lives as well as the lives of others.

Are you ready to dream big, find your purpose, and fuel your burning desire? David will share how you can conceive, believe and achieve your burning desire, your *Life Purpose*.

Many of us have a *Scarcity Mindset as a result of our upbringing and lack of financial education.* To *Live Ready*, you must develop a *Readiness Mindset*. David's 7 gears will help you create a *Readiness Mindset*.

- **Going the Extra Mile**
- **Personal Initiative**
- **Self-Discipline**
- **Controlled Attention**
- **Controlled Enthusiasm**
- **Accurate Thought**
- **Creative Vision**

He reveals the difference between your conscious and subconscious minds, both scientifically and spiritually. Your subconscious mind is a canvas, and your conscious mind is the painter. What a perfect analogy. His advice, "All you have to do is refuse to think about what you don't want, and instead, focus on everything you do want, with as much passion and burning desire as you can generate."

But fear holds people back from achieving the success they deserve. After Hill released *Think and Grow Rich* in 1937, he wrote the manuscript *Outwitting the Devil* in 1938 to address overcoming that fear. Intended to be the sequel to *Think and Grow Rich*, however the title frightened his wife, so it was not published. Instead, the manuscript was locked away for over 70 years. I was honored to be asked to annotate the manuscript and share it with the world in 2011. It reveals Hill's concept of *drifting*. A drifter does not use his or her own mind, they "go with the flow" and as a result seldom find any purpose to their life.

In *Live Ready®–Beyond Think and Grow Rich*, David shares, "Numerous studies have shown through the years that only 3% of people are driven by *Life Purpose*. They are the *Pure Non-Drifters*, as first defined by Napoleon Hill nearly a century ago."

To become a Pure Non-Drifter, follow the guidance in *Live Ready®*. Your Readiness Mindset will become your Success Mindset, you will shed your fear and move forward with faith and courage to achieve the success you so richly deserve!

To Your Success!

Sharon Lechter is the author of *Think and Grow Rich for Women*. Co-author of *Three Feet From Gold, Success and Something Greater, New York Times* Bestseller *Rich Dad Poor Dad* and 14 other *Rich Dad* books. Annotator of *Outwitting the Devil*. **www.sharonlechter.com**

"Some men see things as they are and say why, I dream things that never were and say, why not."

— ROBERT F. KENNEDY

CHAPTER ONE

The Power of Thought

CLOSE YOUR EYES FOR A MOMENT, AND IMAGINE AN eighteen-year-old boy, scrubbing dishes at the back of a restaurant, lonely, nearly broke, and barely able to pay his rent.

Fast-forward three decades. Now, see this boy as a man who owns several businesses and has the power to help thousands of people, worldwide, achieve their goals.

Those are both versions of me, David R. Ibarra. My journey started as a kid headed in the wrong direction. I was convinced that success was not for me. I felt angry and afraid. Today, the picture is 100% different. I know what it takes to overcome doubt, confusion, and fear. I've learned to replace doubtful, negative feelings with positive feelings, images, and goals. I now know what it takes to *Live Ready*® for new challenges and opportunities.

The *Live Ready*® concept embraces the wisdom of world-renowned teachers and leaders like Dr. Napoleon Hill and Dr. José Antonio Calzada. It's also built on my own philosophies, developed during decades of continual practice through the ups and downs of life. *Living Ready* means continual improvement in several core life principles, so that no matter what difficulties you face, you can enjoy life, overcome your challenges, and get what you want.

It took me over 30 years to learn to *Live Ready*®. I stumbled many times and made needless mistakes. I don't want you to have to go through the same thing. I don't want you to have to wait decades or even years to learn the secrets. I want success for you sooner rather than later. How soon you achieve your life goals depends on how faithfully you apply these principles. All you have to do is read this book and *work on it*.

People enter this life into one of two GPS-like thought setting environments. The first is the *Positive-State-of-Mind* joy thought setting, which leads us to the path of *Rewards*. The second is the *Negative-State-of-Mind* fear thought setting, which leads down the path of *Penalties*.

A *Positive-State-of-Mind* looks for ways for you to realize anything you desire. It allows you to focus on what you want, how you're going to acquire it, and the benefits you'll enjoy both while on the journey and once you've achieved your goal, objective, or *Life Purpose*.

A *Negative-State-of-Mind* looks for all the reasons why something can't be done. It's usually the path of least resistance and comes with negative consequences. It prevents you from achieving your goals.

Living Ready starts with the thoughts you allow into your subconscious. Most people don't understand they have the power to choose their own thoughts. Still, securing control of your future begins by acknowledging, accepting, and embracing the *power of your every thought*. The thoughts that occupy your mind are the same ones that develop your positive or negative thought setting, leading you to failure or preparing you to *Live Ready*® for success.

To understand *the Power of Thought*, let me introduce you to the *Brain Model*.

TAKEAWAYS

Living Ready starts with the thoughts you allow into your subconscious.

THE BRAIN MODEL PART ONE
The Power of Your Every Thought

The *Brain Model* teaches you how to control your thoughts, so you can get what you want in life. As you become familiar with the process of controlling your thoughts, you develop a *Rhythm of Success*, and that rhythm will build a *Habit of Success*.

To tap into the full potential of your *Thought-Power*, you need to understand how your brain processes thought. Imagine looking at your brain floating in front of you. The way the brain manages thought is divided into three sections: the sub-conscious (*eighty percent*), the conscious (*fifteen percent*), and the imagination (*five percent*).

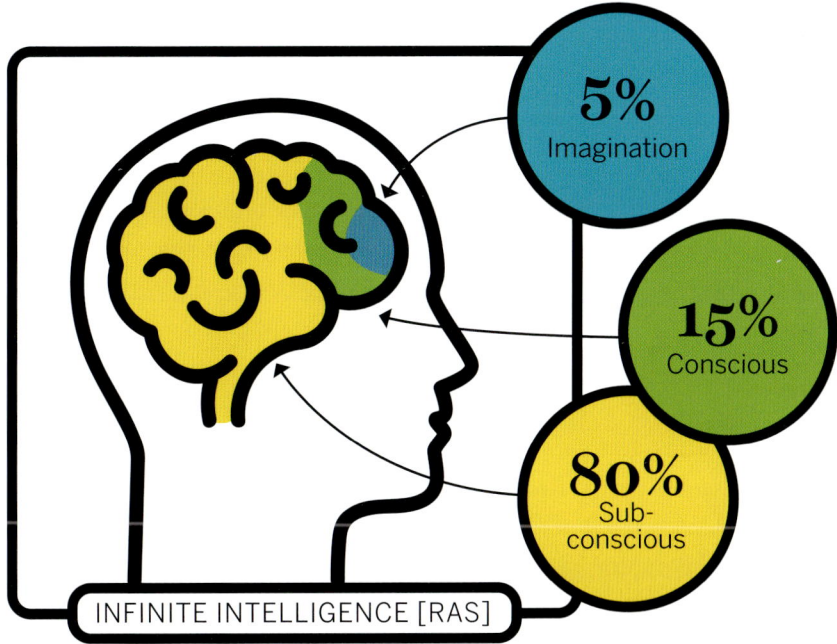

Each of these thought processing sections of the brain have different jobs. The eighty-percent section is your subconscious mind. Your subconscious controls actions you, most likely, are not even aware of, like keeping your lungs working, your heart beating, and your blood flowing. But it does much more: *it also obeys the thoughts you give it*—in other words—***it does whatever you tell it to do.***

Beyond Think and Grow Rich   **17**

That's where your conscious mind comes in. It makes up about fifteen percent of your *Thought-Power*. This part of your mind is driven by the thoughts you feed it daily, whether those thoughts are good or bad, positive, or negative. The thoughts that you allow into your conscious mind seed your subconscious with commands of what to do. Those are the thoughts your subconscious acts on.

If you *think you can,* that's a conscious positive thought that is fed into your subconscious mind. The subconscious takes it as a command and makes it real. And magically, you can!

Similarly, if you *think you can't, you can't.* That's because the subconscious mind takes the negative command from the conscious mind and makes it real. Henry Ford said it best: "If you think you can, you are correct. If you think you can't, you are also correct." Now we come to the last five percent of your brain. This section represents your imagination, and this is where all the action happens. There are two types of imagination: joy, and fear.

Can you guess which one accompanies the *Success Mindset* space? When you're in a *Positive-State-of-Mind,* you believe. You imagine things you have never dreamed possible, and you say to yourself, "Why not me? I can do that." When you believe in yourself, you feel joy.

The *Rewards* are incredible. If you're living with a *Success Mindset,* it's easy to slip into the *Rhythm of Success,* so you can catch new opportunities and create circumstances that lead to more success. This includes *Living Ready* for vibrant physical and mental health, financial independence, peace of mind, enduring friendships, and satisfying personal relationships.

It's also about finding a labor of love that you can express yourself through. When you're living in a *Success Mindset* it's impossible to feel fear, so you move forward with courage. You understand yourself and others, you're immune to all forms of self-limitation, and you choose a happy, well-balanced lifestyle that often leads to prosperity and longevity. If

TAKEAWAYS

If you want complete protection against fear, worry, and stress, living in a **Positive-State-of-Mind** is always the best option.

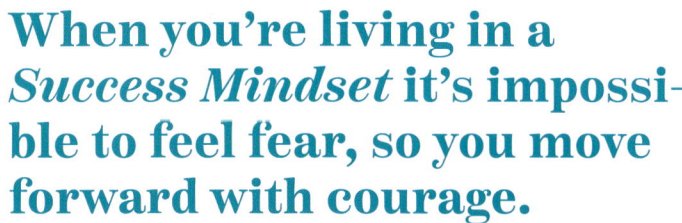

When you're living in a *Success Mindset* it's impossible to feel fear, so you move forward with courage.

you want complete protection against fear, worry, and stress, living in a *Positive-State-of-Mind* is always the best option.

When Negative comes knocking, you experience the complete opposite. The *Negative-State-of-Mind* imagines feelings of fear that block your ability to truly believe in yourself. When negative emotions enter your thoughts, Dr. Doubt whispers to you, "You can't do it," or "You're not good enough." Dr. Doubt's goal is to lock your brain, paralyzing you so you can't move forward.

In a *Negative-State-of-Mind*, there are seven basic fears that can trap you: the fears of not having enough money, criticism, the loss of health, the loss of love, old age, the loss of spare time, and even the fear of death itself. If you entertain thoughts and feelings of fear, eventually you'll end up in the *Negative Nuthouse*. Once inside, it's crowded, and it's difficult to get out.

These fears lead to the *Penalties* associated with a *Negative-State-of-Mind*. Consider the income challenges that people with a negative mindset face. They're usually not happy people. They often develop mind-body limitations, and they impose other limitations upon themselves, because they create an expectation of mediocrity.

People with a *Negative-State-of-Mind* often dislike their occupations, but they're too afraid to change careers. They worry a lot, and this sets them up to be victims of negative influencers who control or manipulate them. It seems like more people dislike them, because they operate with an unpleasant personality, and most positive people just don't want to be around them. There's a sense of desperation, as if life is not and can never be as good as it should be. Fear, in all its negative, controlling forms, reigns like a tyrant, so people with a *Negative-State-of-Mind* never truly feel free or happy.

Whether you're in a *Positive State of Mind* or a negative one, the *Law of Attraction* principle of 'like attracts like' is fully at play. The thoughts you choose to think seem to create a force field around your subconscious, and they invite similar thoughts to enter.

Like a magnet, negative thoughts attract more negative thoughts and experiences, while positive thoughts attract more positive thoughts and experiences. This is because your subconscious mind—the 80% of your *Thought-Power* that lies beneath your conscious thought—is always trying to validate what you choose to think about consistently.

At the same time, the imagination is controlled by the detection of positive or negative emotions. It works like a motion detector that turns a light on or off. Positive and negative emotions are detected by your brain moving you into a *Negative-State-of-Mind* or a *Positive-State-of-Mind*, back and forth, again and again. Our imagination determines, based on the positive or negative emotions it picks up, whether to attract more positive or more negative. The brighter and more prominent your positive emotions are, the easier it is to put your imagination to work for you.

The mystical power of becoming the *Switch Master of Your Own Thought*® lies in taking responsibility for the thoughts you think. It is how you choose which emotions you entertain, the outcomes you imagine, that determine your end-result—good or bad.

You might think this easier said than done, because we all experience challenges, heartaches, and stress, and sometimes it seems like those emotions last forever. However, even in those moments, there is a way to get out of a *Negative-State-of-Mind*, and it's easier than you might think.

When Dr. Doubt whispers to you, take control. Immediately think of something that makes you happy, something you believe in—whether it's the birth of your child, or a book club you belong to, or the outcome of a sporting event.

TAKEAWAYS

Like a magnet, negative thoughts attract more negative thoughts and experiences, while positive thoughts attract more positive thoughts and experiences.

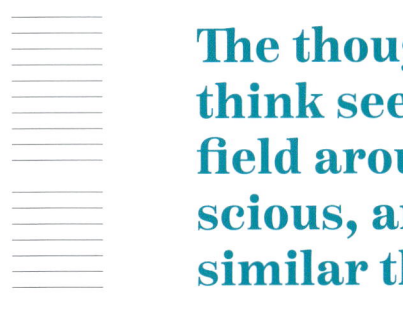

The thoughts you choose to think seem to create a force field around your subconscious, and they invite similar thoughts to enter.

Latch on to whatever makes you smile, because negative thoughts can't occupy a mind filled with positive thoughts. When you focus on a happy thought, the door to the *Negative Nuthouse* opens. Now all you must do is walk out, and slam the door shut behind you.

That's the power of gratitude in action, and it's the power of choice at work. When you allow your positive thoughts to dominate your conscious mind, and you bring them up repeatedly, your subconscious mind responds. Your imagination ignites with a burning desire to show you what you could be, and your subconscious does everything it can to make that dream a reality. It spurs you to action, and you begin to experience success in its most primal, dynamic, and sophisticated form.

The more you use the *Brain Model* to achieve a *Success Mindset*, the more powerful it becomes.

Nothing extraordinary has ever been achieved without a *Positive-State-of-Mind*. What actions should be taken to develop a *Success Mindset* and achieve a *Rhythm of Success?*

It's clear that the first step is recognizing that your *State-of-Mind* is the one and only thing over which you, and you alone, have complete control. As you exercise your ability to choose positive, happy thoughts over negative ones, you learn to close the door to *Negative-State-of-Mind* experiences, cleansing your mind of fear and doubt.

Repetition while in a *Positive-State-of-Mind* lays the foundation of *Living Ready* for success. If you were born into a *Positive-State-of-Mind* thought setting environment, switching negative thoughts to positive ones might come naturally for you. However, if you were born into a

Negative-State-of-Mind thought setting environment, it might take some practice for positive thoughts to become comfortable or familiar, so you can achieve the *Rhythm of Success* and eventually the *Habit of Success*.

So, in summary—eighty percent of your brain is your subconscious. Your subconscious has just one job—to do whatever your thoughts tell it to do. Fifteen percent of your brain is your conscious. Your conscious is your conductor, your driver; it seeds your thoughts into your subconscious, telling it what to do, and your subconscious finds a way to make it a reality—good or bad.

Think of your subconscious as a canvas and your conscious as the painter. Some thoughts are made with weak strokes and inferior paints, fading with time. Some thoughts are painted with the highest quality paints and the strokes of a true artist. These canvases, these thoughts, and habits, become a permanent fixture in your mind, hung up in the house of your thoughts.

On top of your *conscious* is the five percent of your brain that is your imagination—that is where all the action happens. Ideas form from the imagination of either joy or fear.

Remember, joy is felt while in a *Positive-State-of-Mind*—when you believe. Fear is felt while in a *Negative-State-of-Mind*—when you disbelieve. Your imagination is controlled by the detection of positive or negative emotions. It works like a motion detector that turns a light on or off. Positive and negative emotions are detected by your brain moving you into a *Negative-State-of-Mind* or a *Positive-State-of-Mind*.

If you are negative—you disbelieve—and a negative force field encircles your subconscious. While in a *Negative-State-of-Mind*, negative attracts negative. Then like a magnet, the subconscious tries to validate your negative thought and drag more negative thoughts into it. You think, "I don't believe I can do this, or something will happen to cause me to fail." Whether it is true or not, the subconscious will try to validate the disbelief and make it a reality. The paint fades, and soon there are piles of incomplete or unused canvases filling your subconscious.

TAKEAWAYS

Remember, **joy** is felt while in a *Positive-State-of-Mind*—when you believe. **Fear** is felt while in a *Negative-State-of-Mind*—when you disbelieve.

THE BRAIN MODEL **PART TWO**
The DOSE Chemicals

The *Brain Model* isn't fiction. The mystical, powerful, and dynamic power of thought is supported by science—and that science is linked to positive emotions like love and gratitude.

On a biological level, positive emotions translate into positive chemicals. A positive thought, coupled with a positive emotion, releases beneficial neurotransmitters in the brain that impact the entire body. More importantly, these chemicals—the DOSE chemicals—support the maintenance of a *Positive-State-of-Mind*.

DOSE is an acronym using the first letter of four types of positive neurotransmitters: dopamine, oxytocin, serotonin, and endorphins. Each of these neurotransmitters has its place in the sense of completeness and purpose you feel as you work on your goals, objectives, or *Life Purpose*.

Dopamine is often called 'the happiness chemical.' This hormone controls feel-good emotions, like anticipation and the desire for a positive outcome. It's responsible for the wonderful, elated feeling that occurs every time you achieve something.

Dopamine also helps create the *Rhythm of Success*, which evolves into the *Habit of Success*. It makes you want to chase after the feel-good state that comes with an accomplishment. When you learn to use dopamine correctly, you allow it to reward you internally for actions completed to achieve your goals, objectives, or *Life Purpose*. This builds the desire to work on those actions again and again, giving you the feeling of accomplishment and propelling you forward, so you can *Live Ready*® for both challenges and success.

If you're using it incorrectly, dopamine can create habits of checking social media too often, or even of getting addicted to video games. The tiny bursts of dopamine that occur with each achievement, real or imagined, can be monitored, and trained to help you stay on track.

Oxytocin, another powerful neurotransmitter, is often called 'the bonding hormone.' Oxytocin is responsible for the wonderful rush of closeness that people feel when they spend time together, particularly when the element of touch is involved. This is the chemical that is released in a mother's body when she holds a newborn baby, when two people who are in love cuddle with each other, when young children with scraped knees run to an adult to wipe away their tears and hug away the heart-hurt, or even when people release tension through acupressure or a massage. Touch isn't always necessary for the release of oxytocin, but it can amplify it.

Oxytocin's overall job is to give us the ability to understand other people, to develop empathy for them, and then to act in both wisdom and compassion. It enhances our ability to trust and work harmoniously as a team with other people.

Serotonin regulates our moods, both good and bad. It's responsible for stabilizing those moods. Serotonin helps provide feelings of calmness, contentedness, and emotional well-being. This helps us maintain a *Success Mindset*. Serotonin also impacts our sleep, our digestion, and communication between neurons, so that the entire body is grounded in health and wellness. This gives our minds the ability to focus on important issues.

Endorphins are good-feeling endurance chemicals. These are the hormones that are released when you're running a marathon, providing you with a runner's high that pushes you past your limits. Endorphins help you play through pain so you can reach your goals, objectives, or *Life Purpose*. They provide feelings of euphoria and wellbeing, the sense of happiness that develops a burning desire to work hard to make your dreams come true.

When the DOSE chemicals are working together, they can help you maintain a *Success Mindset*. They keep you focused on your purpose, enjoying the journey, so you take *Faith-Based Action* to get what you want.

You'll still have to ignore Dr. Doubt's whispered invitation to his *Negative Nuthouse*. Negativity is a byproduct of stress. Under the right circumstances, a small burst of stress can help you reach your goals. However, if you're under too much stress for too long, the stress hormone called cortisol builds up in your body.

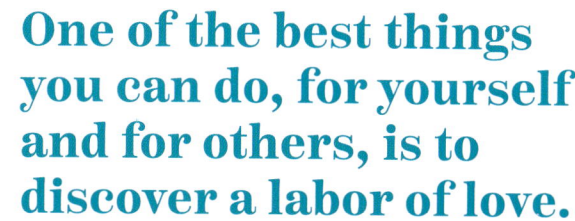

One of the best things you can do, for yourself and for others, is to discover a labor of love.

This negatively impacts health in many ways. It keeps you in fight-or-flight mode, so getting deep, rejuvenating rest becomes difficult. It affects insulin sensitivity, leading to weight gain and lifestyle diseases such as diabetes and heart disease. Literally, too much cortisol makes you sick.

The release of cortisol is a natural process. It's not something that you can control, but you can slow its release by pivoting to a *Positive-State-of-Mind* when you begin to feel negative.

Once you're back in that *Success Mindset*, you begin releasing DOSE chemicals that help create and maintain positive thoughts. Positive attracts positive. As you begin to seed your mind with positive thoughts, you become a believer in your own potential. You begin to focus on your goals, objectives, or *Life Purpose* to get what you want.

When you have a written goal, objective, or a *Life Purpose*, and you direct your energy into it, then you have the basis for building a *Success Mindset* that allows you to release those DOSE chemicals.

If you don't know what you want, you could start by defining what 'Rich' means to you. Analyze the areas of family/friends, faith, community, health, and financial wealth, and how these areas form unique combinations of joy in your life. Then set up a plan to acquire or experience those things that make you, personally, feel rich and happy.

While you're focusing on what you need to achieve your definition of rich, give some of your attention to forming a habit of gratitude to those that make you feel good. Your expression of gratitude will make them feel good, in return. This easy action only takes a few moments of your time, and it is a great catalyst for releasing oxytocin and other good-feeling chemicals in the brain. Drop a note of encouragement through text, email, or a social media message, or call someone and give them a verbal high-five. Open the door for someone. Let the other car go first in traffic. These small acts of kindness stack up in unexpected ways. Often, you will form a strong *Success Mindset* because expressing these small forms of gratitude helps you gain the *Rhythm of Success*. When you 'give-give-give, before you get-get-get,' you receive a boost of DOSE chemicals to help guide you.

One of the best things you can do, for yourself and for others, is to discover a labor of love. Find a passion, your *Life Purpose*, and get to work achieving it. Apply your whole heart and soul. When you're completely engaged in something you enjoy, there's no room for Dr. Doubt's negative whispers to be heard, and you will offer valuable service to other people in the process. It's also a great way to engage in *Faith-Based Action* that rewards you with bursts of dopamine as you work toward your goals, objectives, or *Life Purpose*.

Part of eliminating negative emotions means repairing relationships when you can. Make a list of people you may have unjustly offended and reach out sincerely to apologize and ask for forgiveness. This can be a bitter task, but once you've done all you can do to make things right, you can walk away with your head held high, no matter what the outcome is.

As you work on repairing the divides between you and other people, it will become clear that no one—NO ONE—has the power to hurt your feelings, make you angry, or frighten you. You are the only person who can control your thoughts. You have the power to discard the negative seeds that others try to plant in your subconscious. As you maintain a *Success Mindset,* the DOSE chemicals work together to help you move past any hurt or negative emotions you may have felt in the past.

TAKEAWAYS

When you're completely engaged in something you enjoy, there's no room for **Dr. Doubt's negative whispers** to be heard.

THE BRAIN MODEL PART THREE
The Reticular Activating System (RAS)

Tens of thousands of signals are sent to the brain every second, through a complex chain of neurons. These signals come from all over the body. Information comes through our senses—sight, sound, smell, taste, and the sensation of touch—as well as through the function of specific organs, including our lungs, heart, digestive system and every thought we think.

The sheer volume of data is more than our minds can handle. The brain can only process around 130 thought signals per second. To manage the information, our brains are equipped with a way to filter through these signals. This filtering mechanism is known as the reticular activating system, or RAS.

The RAS sorts this information and then routes it to the proper place in the mind, where it can be interpreted. If it weren't for the RAS, our brains would be flooded with data. We would be too overwhelmed to make decisions.

The RAS utilizes the *brain model* to determine what information we accept, including what we're aware of in any given moment. We adjust the setting for our RAS depending on what we believe and what we focus on.

Have you ever begun the shopping process, and suddenly, you see the advertising and billboards everywhere for the product you are interested in? That's the RAS at work. The same phenomenon occurs when you buy something you've wanted for a long time, and then suddenly, you notice a better deal on a similar product, after you've already made the purchase.

The RAS also impacts our ability to see new opportunities for reaching our goals, objectives, or *Life Purpose*. Many times, these opportunities are unexpected. They can seem to pop up out of the blue, or they can show up in circumstances we never anticipated. The RAS is fully equipped to help us find exciting new ways to make progress to get what we want.

Although we're not consciously aware of it, the RAS also

discards information that we subconsciously disagree with. We like to believe that our thinking is always accurate and rational. However, the things we notice and the information we're aware of are always selectively filtered through the RAS.

The RAS often blocks information that does not match our beliefs, emotions, or desires. It can prevent us from seeing information we don't agree with. This can be good or bad. If our information is based on *Accurate Thought*, our RAS can focus on the actions that will ensure we achieve our goals, objectives, or *Life Purpose*.

If we have programmed our RAS with inaccurate thought, our RAS can take us down a path that can prevent us from getting what we want. Therefore, it is important to condition your RAS to challenge the accuracy of your thought, to achieve your desired end results. The good news is that the RAS can be trained by the conscious thoughts you choose to think, so you can remain open to important information.

The RAS does a good job allowing all the information we need for our survival to come to our attention. Most of the time, we notice when a traffic pattern suddenly switches, so we can be aware and drive safely. We notice changes in the weather that could be potentially dangerous, and we plan. We may even be aware of changes in our heart rate, breathing patterns, or temperature, warning us to rest more, eat better, and get more exercise—that is our RAS at work.

When we meet new people, our RAS can filter our perception of them, allowing us to like them or dislike them, based only on what we notice. We often don't see personality traits or quirks that would impact our perception of them, for good or bad, because we may not have the same beliefs or personality patterns.

On the other hand, if thinking is wired to seek for ways that people are different, the RAS will point out all those quirks and personality differences. This can also impact the way you see people. Sometimes

TAKEAWAYS

The RAS often blocks information that does not match our beliefs, emotions, or desires. This can be good or bad.

> **If our information is based on *Accurate Thought*, our RAS can focus on the actions that will ensure we achieve our goals, objectives, or *Life Purpose*.**

this results in prejudice, and sometimes it results in an open-minded acceptance of people from all walks of life. It depends on the thoughts you think, because that's how you train and set your filtering system.

The interesting thing about the RAS—as it relates to thought—is that it's part of the subconscious mind. Its only objective is to do exactly what we tell it to do: to filter information, based on the things we consciously focus on.

When we're in a *Success Mindset*, and we fix our thoughts upon a goal, objective, or *Life Purpose*, we're beginning to light up the RAS, to adjust the settings the way we want them set. As we consciously direct our thoughts to the *Faith-Based Action* that we need to execute to achieve what we want, we're conditioning our subconscious mind, and shifting the filtering focus of our RAS.

This opens our minds up to new possibilities that support our *Faith-Based Action*. We see opportunities we never would have noticed before. We find time to create habits for small, essential activities that we never took time for in the past. As we stay consciously focused on what we want, the RAS filters the information we receive to show us exactly what we need to know and do to *Live Ready*®—to achieve a *Rhythm of Success* that builds the *Habit of Success*.

Remember, the subconscious mind acts first on the thoughts we allow to dominate our minds. Whether those thoughts are positive or negative, our subconscious minds will act on them. The RAS will filter information to make it easier to carry out those thoughts—good or bad.

Therefore, it's essential to learn to be the *Switch Master of Your Own Thought*® and *Pivot to Positive*®. As you do, you begin to release DOSE chemicals, while at the same time, resetting your RAS. You're seeding your subconscious mind, so you believe in yourself and what you want to achieve.

If you don't take the responsibility to *Pivot to Positive*®, you allow your body to release cortisol. Too much cortisol reinforces negative thoughts. In this case, the RAS begins to filter your perception, so that all you see is negative, and it can become difficult to *Pivot to Positive*®.

From a health standpoint, it's also dangerous. Persistently thinking negative thoughts creates an internal environment where your body is constantly flooded with cortisol. This can lead to adrenal fatigue. Eventually, you may not even want to get out of bed in the morning.

While it's possible to become addicted to your own negative emotions and the chemicals that go with them, your brain craves positive emotions and chemicals. Positive emotions and DOSE chemicals make you feel good, which in turn makes you believe.

Like attracts like. As you learn to turn on those DOSE chemicals and set your RAS to get what you want, you create and maintain a *Success Mindset*. Your focus on your goals, objectives, or *Life Purpose* becomes set, and you begin to *Live Ready*® for everything that comes your way.

THE BRAIN MODEL PART FOUR

Dr. Doubt, The Creator, and Infinite Intelligence

Who do you want whispering to you—Dr. Doubt, the Adversary, who leads you to a *Negative-State-of-Mind* and ultimately failure, or the Creator, who can guide you, when asked to, toward achievement and success?

There is a choice of whom to invite into your subconscious mind. The way you set and train your RAS provides you with a stream of Infinite Intelligence guidance, for either good or bad. This continual flow of intelligence supports your *Habit of Success* to become a *Pure Non-Drifter*, or your habit of failure to become a *Drifter*. It all depends on what you seed into your subconscious and who you choose to listen to—Dr. Doubt—the Adversary, or the Creator.

Close your eyes for a moment and remember what it was like to be a child. Children believe. Their faith makes it easy for them to imagine succeeding at everything they do. As a child, you might have believed that if you put on Superman's cape, you could fly. You might have even believed that a new pair of sneakers could make you run faster than before.

The process of growing up introduces you to your other self: the disbeliever. You're taught to accept that your dreams are just dreams. You begin to accept that the things you want are limited by your circumstances, or sometimes, by what other people tell you.

You begin to think that all your dreams will do is disappoint you, but that is not the way it has to be. The only reason people don't run marathons, or start a successful business, or achieve any other goal, objective, or *Life Purpose*, is because they let the Adversary—Dr. Doubt—whisper to them that they can't.

When negative emotions such as fear, disappointment, or sadness fill your mind, you develop a *Negative-State-of-Mind*. This attracts the penalties reserved for negative thinking, and your subconscious validates Dr. Doubt's whispers, along with his invitation to his *Negative Nuthouse*.

> **One of the greatest gifts that humans possess is the ability to choose the thoughts that occupy our minds.**

While in a *Negative-State-of-Mind* setting, Dr. Doubt, the Adversary, is the *Infinite Intelligence* guiding you. He will seed your subconscious with negative thoughts that will prevent you from getting what you want—thoughts like, "You don't have what it takes to achieve what you want", or "Success was never meant for you."

When this happens, the only opportunities your RAS will present to you are opportunities to fail. And your imagination will seed your subconscious with more negative fear emotions, creating a negative thought setting, to ensure you will not get what you want in life.

The good thing is, you can never be in a *Positive-State-of-Mind* and a *Negative-State-of-Mind* at the same time—and you can choose to *Pivot to Positive*®.

While you're in a *Success Mindset*, the Creator is the *Infinite Intelligence* that can guide you when asked. This type of guidance reminds you that you're worthy of what you want, you're capable of achieving it, and you can enjoy the process of achieving your goals, objectives, or *Life Purpose*.

One of the greatest gifts that humans possess is the ability to choose the thoughts that occupy our minds. If you know how to control your thoughts in a way that creates and maintains a *Success Mindset*, your subconscious mind can become the gateway to *Infinite Intelligence*.

This exceptional gift allows us to tap into a continual stream of intelligence, finding solutions to seemingly unsolvable problems. Oftentimes, this moves us forward toward our goals much faster than we might have thought possible.

There are a few prerequisites for this. First, you need faith to do the things that lead to success. Focus on *Faith-Based Action* to achieve your desired result, while maintaining a *Positive-State-of-Mind*. As you do these things, you reset your RAS. Then, when you make a request, your RAS is primed to find the answers you seek and present them to you in a way that allows you to act upon them.

This set of actions is like sending a formal invitation, welcoming the infinite flow of intelligence into your life. Sometimes, the invitation is all that *Infinite Intelligence* needs.

Consider what happens when you go to bed with a question on your mind, and you wake up halfway through the night with the answer. Think of the times you've been presented with a problem, and while pondering on it, the solution bursts into your mind. Remember the times when you've wondered about the right thing to say, and you almost stumbled over the right words or topic that stimulates an engaging, productive conversation.

There might be times when you're traveling somewhere, and you have a sudden, almost irresistible urge to take a different path than you usually do. Sometimes those off-the-beaten-path journeys present opportunities you could never find otherwise.

These situations can rise in social arenas, in business, and in daily life, in almost any arena. If you're focused on your *Purpose* and living in a *Success Mindset*, this type of intelligence can flow into your subconscious mind every moment, when called upon.

The question is, what type of ideas do you want flowing into your life? Do you want the creative, *Infinite Intelligence* of the Creator flowing through you, or the dark whispers of Dr. Doubt?

The choice is clear. If you become the *Switch Master of Your Own Thought*® and *Pivot to Positive*®, you will have the flow of intelligence and guidance from the Creator to help you achieve your goals. This is one of the first steps to *Living Ready*.

It won't be easy. Every day, for your entire life, you'll have to fight the disbeliever inside of you. You'll have to avoid the

TAKEAWAYS

If you know how to control your thoughts in a way that creates and maintains a **Success Mindset**, your subconscious mind can become the gateway to **Infinite Intelligence.**

Beyond Think and Grow Rich 33

whispers of Dr. Doubt by fiercely guiding your conscious thoughts, so they can direct your subconscious and your imagination.

Only a few people experience the true *Pure Non-Drifter* life, *Living Ready* for both challenges and success. If you want to run a marathon, or a business, or achieve any other great dream, then you've got to realize you're the *Switch Master of Your Own Thought*®, *Pivot to Positive*®, and begin to control your own *State-of-Mind*.

Do you need permission? If so, I'm granting it to you right now, but it's your decision that counts. Give yourself the permission to build and maintain a *Success Mindset*. Believe in yourself, believe in what you want to accomplish. When you do, you will regain the power, the faith, and the energy you were born with, so you can do whatever you want to do.

Fill your mind with thoughts of faith, joy, and the idea that success is your right. Your RAS will latch onto these ideas. Your subconscious mind and your imagination will go to work for you, and you will attract the rewards of these positive thoughts.

You are the only one who can change your thought setting. You can choose the *Drifter's* habit of mediocrity, or the *Pure Non-Drifter's* habit that creates a beautiful *Rhythm of Success*. You can either use your brain to control your thinking and build the life you want, or you can let Dr. Doubt's whispers distract you. Following the *Live Ready*® principles is ALWAYS up to you.

To illustrate how the *Brain Model* works to achieve both BAD and GOOD, I would like to share the story of Dave Durocher.

TAKEAWAYS

You are the only one who can change your thought setting. You can choose the *Drifter's* habit of mediocrity, or the *Pure Non-Drifter's* habit that creates a beautiful *Rhythm of Success*.

Even the most broken people can reinvent themselves and become somebody they have never known. It does not matter if they have lived their life on the street, been a life-long drug addict, or spent their life in jails and prisons. Anyone can change.

It was a normal night for Dave Durocher. He was headed to a friend's house to weigh up some dope for sale and to get high. As Dave was driving, he looked out the window

> **You can either use your brain to control your thinking and build the life you want, or you can let Dr. Doubt's whispers distract you.**

and spotted a helicopter hovering high up in the sky. Because Dave had other things on his mind, he just continued to drive, not thinking much of the helicopter. After all, it really did not appear to be going anywhere. Dave entered the drug house, got high, and then prepared his batch of cocaine to sell. After a couple of hours, the time of the night was right, and Dave was ready to hit the streets, to have what he considered fun, do some damage, and make some money.

As Dave hopped into his car, he turned on some tunes and pulled out onto the street. At that moment, he saw in his rearview mirror what seemed like a hundred cop cars, all in hot pursuit of him with their sirens blaring. The helicopter from earlier was now hovering just above him, shining its spotlight into his car, making it almost impossible to drive. A dominant thought rushed into Dave's mind: after his last stint in prison, he promised himself that if he ever got chased by the police again, he would not stop. Dave knew that if they caught him, he would spend the rest of his life in prison. Another thought ran through his brain: there was only one thing that was going to stop him today, and that was a bullet. Dave took those police officers on a high-speed chase. It was a hairy and hectic moment. Dave drove with absolutely no regard for public safety. The thought continued to rage through his mind, "You're going to have to kill me—I am not going back to prison—so game on—come and get me!"

Then Dave remembered there was a bridge ahead. If he could get there, he could throw the dope out the window and into the water.

Maybe, he could still get out of this mess. As Dave came around the corner heading for the bridge, he gunned it. Then he saw it—a roadblock. Now, he knew he had a decision to make, though he quickly realized he had already made the decision. He hunkered down and accelerated, thinking that he'd run the roadblock and commit suicide by police shooting. But to Dave's surprise, no shots were fired. As Dave turned, the cop behind him performed a PIT maneuver, spinning him out of control. Dave crashed into an embankment. Before Dave could get out of the car and go on the attack, he was pulled out of the car, handcuffed, and then taken into custody.

A few days later, Dave sat in jail, realizing he was facing a 29-year prison sentence, meaning he would spend the rest of his life behind bars. Dave was devastated. He did not know what to do, but he knew he had to do something different. He could not continue living his life this way.

For the first time in Dave's life, he felt the desire to change. It was then he recalled Delancey Street, a place he heard about during his previous time behind bars. Delancey Street was an alternative to prison for guys just like Dave, who didn't know how to live right and had to learn or relearn everything there was about how to live a good, law-abiding, value-centered life.

Dave decided to write to the Delancey Street Foundation in the hopes of getting an interview for recommended acceptance to possibly avoid his 29-year prison sentence. The interview day came, and Dave did his best to con his way into the program, but, to Dave's disappointment, he was rejected. Dave felt pure despair with the rejection. However, he had nothing to lose, so he wrote them another letter. They came and interviewed Dave for a second time. This time, Dave pleaded for their help, which resulted in him being accepted to the program. Now Dave had to hope that the judge would sentence him to Delancey Street rather than prison.

Dave's court day arrived. He sat in the cage, shackled, as the judge entered, and all stood. The judge addressed Dave.

"Mr. Durocher, against my better judgment, I am going to sentence you to Delancey Street on one condition. You are going to plead guilty today to 22-years. That way, when you get kicked out or split, I've got you for the rest of your life!"

Dave couldn't sign the plea bargain fast enough. The first thought that came to Dave was that it didn't really matter what Delancey Street was, because it was two years of his life rather than 22.

During the year Dave spent in jail waiting for the legal process to play out, he had time to think—really think. How did his life get this way? Dave realized then that he got everything he thought of and that every thought he created became his reality. And now, for the very first time, Dave felt a strong desire to really do something different. Dave really wanted to change. He was broken, tired, and he was scared. Dave knew prison would not help him; he had done it four times already. He also knew a simple 30-to-90-day drug program would not help him either. Dave realized he was too damaged and stuck in his destructive lifestyle habits for a program like that to do him any good. He knew he needed something more drastic. And the one thing Dave knew about Delancey Street was that it was drastic!

Delancey Street creates the structure that begins when the student asks for help. They know that change cannot occur until the person applying to get into the program has the desire to want help. When Dave reached that point, Delancey Street accepted him because he took the first step to accept help—he asked for it.

Dave learned to reseed his mind by doing—acting as if he was honest until he became honest. He acted as if he was accountable until he became accountable. Dave learned to do the right thing every single day for hundreds of days in a row until it became his belief. Dave experienced a paradigm shift; he recalibrated his moral compass. When Dave completed his required two years at Delancey Street, he requested and was granted the opportunity to stay an additional year. Over those three years he replaced his bad habits with good habits. He became a believer in himself and what he and Delancey Street had to offer others who had lost their way.

By the end of Dave's three years at Delancey Street, Dave was running the entire facility, overseeing 250 students and 15 vocational training schools. These schools generated millions of dollars every

The power of your every thought encompasses the things you say, do, and believe. It impacts your ability to *Live Ready*®.

year to help fund the entire operation, so Delancey Street could continue to help people turn their lives around without charging them a dime, no matter how long they had to stay in the program.

This became the most significant accomplishment in Dave's entire life, up until launching *The Other Side Academy* in Salt Lake City, Utah—which is fashioned after Delancey Street.

Dave spent the first half of his life helping to destroy people, and now he is spending the second half saving them.

Dave Durocher's story is a powerful example of how he seeded his subconscious with a *Positive-State-of-Mind* thought setting to turn his life around, as well as the lives of thousands of others.

You either use your brain to control your thoughts to *Live Ready*® and get the things you want, or you allow Dr. Doubt's uninvited whispers to seed your subconscious and grow a crop of negative thinking that will produce things you do not want. You have a choice in this situation: You can take control of your *Thought-Power*, or you can let it be influenced by the whispers of doubt that create the circumstances that you do not want. It really is all up to you—it is your choice!

In the following chapter, you will learn in more detail about the power of knowing what you want: a goal, objective, or *Life Purpose*.

Summary:

The circumstances you were born into don't matter as much as your ability to control your thoughts. The power of your every thought encompasses the things you say, do, and believe. It impacts your ability to *Live Ready*®.

As you learn to control and utilize the *Brain Model*, you gain the ability to pivot to a *Positive-State-of-Mind* setting. This allows you to release positive neurotransmitters in the brain known as DOSE chemicals. The DOSE chemicals keep you in a *Success Mindset,* allowing your reticular activation system to discover new opportunities for growth. As you become attuned to the positive guidance of *Infinite Intelligence*, you experience continued success—and you start to Live Ready®.

Power of Thought *challenge*

Access QR code or at eleadertech.com/BMV

"When you find your WHY, you don't hit snooze no more! You find a way to make it happen!"

— ERIC THOMAS

CHAPTER TWO

The Power of Purpose

PURPOSE IS THE STARTING POINT OF ALL ACHIEVEMENT. *Nothing happens until you know what you want.* Remember this, for it is an inescapable truth.

The game of life cannot be won without having a *Life Purpose*. Amazingly, most people live their lives without having a defined purpose in life, so they never really get what they could and should have. What is your *Life Purpose*? In this chapter, together we will begin the process to discover it.

Numerous studies have shown through the years that only 3% of people are driven by a *Life Purpose*. They are the *Pure Non-Drifters*, as first defined by Napoleon Hill nearly a century ago. That means 97% of all people lack a *Life Purpose*. They suffer from mild to severe levels of drifting. *Drifters* stagnate and settle for wherever life takes them, whatever job comes along and whatever fate has in store for them. If you want to be in this group, I suggest you stop reading this book now and go take a nice long nap.

Over the last twenty years, I have researched thousands of people from all walks of life and have found the statistics identified in Dr. Hill's research have not changed much.

The 3% Pure Non-Drifters—entered this world predominantly into a pure *Positive-State-of-Mind* environment setting. Through faith and inspiration—either in themselves or a higher power—they find their *Life Purpose* early. They develop a burning desire to succeed at something very specific. Steve Jobs, founder of Apple, believed he could put a computer in every human hand at a time when no one thought it possible. Jeff Bezos, founder of Amazon, saw the day when everyone could shop online for almost anything—this at a time when everyone shopped at a brick-and-mortar store. Elon Musk, CEO of Tesla, and founder of SpaceX thought cars should be electric and driverless at a time when all cars had to have a driver and ran on gasoline. He also thinks humans will one day inhabit other planets.

There are thousands of these *Pure Non-Drifters* all around the world—people who are achieving their *Purpose* simply because they are crystal clear on what they want. They understand the *Power of Purpose. They know they will succeed no matter what.* These achievers have written goals and actions they recite several times a day. They track their progress and make required changes when needed to stay on path.

Pure Non-Drifters are purpose-driven dreamers, and their aim is to reinvent the future. They hunt for things to improve. These *Pure Non-Drifters* seek out problems. They ask questions that others would be uncomfortable asking. They know that finding solutions to these questions will lead them down a path toward *Rewards*.

Three-percent people are true visionaries, with the Big Ideas of their time. They realize change is mandatory, and that the only thing optional in life is one's own improvement. They live for challenges. Three-percenters are essentially children who live in adult bodies. They still get excited, and they find it difficult to calm down.

Many may look at these "purpose-driven" people who are full of enthusiasm, and say, "Gee, they're weird." But if you are a

TAKEAWAYS

Purpose is the starting point of all achievement. Nothing happens until you know what you want. Remember this, for it is an inescapable truth.

The game of life cannot be won without having a *Life Purpose*

three-percenter, it's fun to be weird. People in the 3% group are natural leaders. They are life's change-makers.

The 10% Partial Drifters—entered this world predominantly into a partial *Positive-State-of-Mind* environment setting. People in this group are problem solvers. They take great pride in their problem-solving abilities, and they welcome the opportunity to showcase this talent.

While they are solving problems, they connect to a *Success Mindset* to achieve solutions. Once problems are solved, they often start to drift while waiting for their next assignment. While they receive many of life's *Rewards*, they also pay *Penalties* for the time they spend drifting.

This 10% group are often managers, integrators, and *Specialized Talent Team* members. One characteristic of the ten-percenter is they often won't react as quickly as three-percenters. They often need an emergency before they take action.

The 60% Natural Drifters—entered this world predominantly into a natural *Negative-State-of-Mind* environment setting. They were obedient. When they were told to settle down, they settled down. When they were told to calm down, they calmed down. They lost the child that once lived inside them. They fight the urge of getting excited to protect themselves from disappointment. They were taught that success was not meant for them.

Sixty-percenters are not self-directed, and this makes them *drift*. They lack *Purpose*, vision, and the ability to dream.

On any Monday morning, you can ask them, "How are you?" they will reply, "Well okay, considering it's a Monday," or in the middle of the week, "Great. It's Wednesday, hump day, I've only got two more days to go till the weekend."

This group plans their whole year around their allotted vacation time. Their goal is to simply get through the day, the week, the month, hoping they will find happiness once they retire. They hide from problems, hoping somehow the problems will go away on their own, so they do not get blamed for them.

If a positive goal enters the mind of a sixty-percenter, the uninvited whispers of Dr. Doubt quickly introduce them to one or more of the seven basic fears. This causes them to pivot to a *Negative-State-of-Mind*, and they become disbelievers. This group often finds themselves living paycheck to paycheck, in constant fear of not having enough money.

Sixty-percenters often want to belong to something bigger than themselves. They want to feel like they matter, and when inspired by a *Pure Non-Drifter*, they can become excellent team members.

The 27% Destructive Drifters

—entered this world predominantly into a destructive *Negative-State-of-Mind* environment setting. Their goal in life is to get something for nothing. They are takers and are unwilling to give in return.

The 27% *Destructive Drifter* does not look for problems to solve, because they ARE the problem. They are dream killers. Their life's purpose is to wreck the companies they work for and to kill the dreams and hopes of others.

Most 27% *Destructive Drifters* are so negative that they cannot be changed. Members of this group should be avoided. If you own a company and you have a 27% person as a team member, you should consider transferring them to your competition so they can wreck that company instead of yours. 27% *Destructive Drifters* are rewarded with life's *Penalties*.

TAKEAWAYS

Surveys have validated that a minimum of **eighty-seven percent of all people are simply drifting through life.**

Now the fact is, most people can display a little bit of the characteristics or actions of each of these four categories, but one of these categories is their dominant setting. While we do not get to choose our original "GPS-like" thought setting, we can learn to reprogram it to get whatever we want in life—if we gain the desire to do so.

Think of it! Surveys have validated that a minimum of eighty-seven percent of all people are simply drifting through life. They are not actively practicing the *Live Ready*® principles, therefore, they lose access to *Rewards* and largely experience the *Penalties* reserved for *Drifters*.

In 2022, it was estimated there were more than 800,000 new small businesses started in the United States. If the previous studies hold true, according to the United States Bureau of Labor Statistics, approximately 20 percent (or around 160,000) will fail by the end of the first year.

Of these new businesses, it is estimated that approximately 50 percent (or 400,000) will fail by the end of five years. By the end of ten years, around 70 percent (or roughly 560,000) will have failed. Only 30 percent (or 240,000) of these businesses will survive 10 years.

Why is there such a high failure rate? Putting it simply, people are starting their business without a *Business Purpose*. Many people who open businesses are trying to escape from someone else's dream, theme, or poorly defined *Business Purpose*. They have not yet fully visualized their own.

This is a high price to pay for not gaining the *Power of Purpose*.

The statistics presented so far should be alarming to you. While there may be those who challenge these statistics, a few hours of online research will show you hundreds of studies validating the percentages of people that are purpose-driven goal-setters and the percentages that drift through their lives without goals or a *Life Purpose*.

The question is, how can you become a goal setter and *Purpose-driven individual*?

Successful businesses and successful people have a lot in common. When we analyze them, it becomes clear why they succeed.

We don't get to choose where we start in life, but we can choose where we end up in life.

Let me introduce my story—the David R. Ibarra *Life Purpose* story.

We don't get to choose where we start in life, but we can choose where we end up in life.

I started life with a very untraditional childhood. I was two years old, and my brother, Mickey, three, when we were entered into the state of Utah foster care system, where we would spend most of the next 13 years.

During this time period, some people in Utah were not very kind to kids of color. The discrimination that I felt made me believe that I didn't matter, that I didn't fit, and that success was not intended for me.

I wanted to leave the foster care system and Utah. I wanted to join my dad, who I held in my mind's eye as my personal hero. Finally, at the age of 14, I was able to move to Sacramento, California and reunite with my father.

Spending the next four years with my father, I learned many things. One, I lived in a community where others looked just like me. I fit in. I didn't stand out. The one thing I could not overcome was the anger that lived inside me. I didn't have a purpose. I didn't have a direction. I had no idea what the future held for me. I was scared. The only thing I did know was I had to do something different.

I enrolled in the Sacramento City Community College, where the tuition was free for everyone. All I had to do was buy my books. I registered for five classes. In the mornings, I had a part-time job as a teller at Wells Fargo bank, in a program for underprivileged youngsters just like me. My time was restricted. I was busier than I had ever been in my life. At night, I had to study, because school was not easy for me: it was work, and hard work.

I found myself short of funds to pay my rent. I needed just $200 more a month to pay my portion of the rent for an apartment I shared with two other friends. I needed to get another part-time job. I needed a job that I could work alone, because by the end of the day, I was both tired and felt brain-dead.

My roommate told me there was a dishwasher job opening at Farrell's Ice Cream Parlour Restaurant, where he was a server. He called the restaurant manager and made an appointment for me to be interviewed. I rushed right down. Just before the interview, I had a thought. What if I didn't qualify? Dr. Doubt, the adversary, was whispering in my ear, and I listened, and became very nervous about interviewing for this position. In spite of my doubts, I got the job, and what I thought would be the most insignificant position in my life became a life changer.

The dish room was wet, slippery, and messy. It was not a fun environment to work in, but I was alone, and that made me happy, until two weeks into the job, when I received a visitor.

My visitor was a man in his early fifties, with slightly gray hair, a handlebar mustache, a red jacket, and a goofy looking, two inch in length, black straight tie that all the male workers at Farrell's wore. The tie was developed so it didn't dip into the ice cream or touch the food. Smart idea, but I thought it still looked goofy.

He entered the dish room. "Hi, young man," he said. "My name is Robert E. Farrell, and I want you to know that you have the most important job of anybody in this restaurant." With that, he stuck his hand out for me to shake.

My hand was covered with food debris from the dirty plates, but he still held his hand out in front of me. I felt self-conscious about my soiled hands, but since he appeared to want to shake, I obliged him, with a smile on my face, as I shook his hand and shared some of the food debris with it.

Mr. Farrell shook my hand firmly. "I can see you're a little hesitant in my belief in the importance of your job, but I mean it—I mean it."

At that point, Mr. Farrell looked at my name tag, and continued. "David, come with me. Let me show you."

We walked to the end of the dining area. The room was full. Every seat was taken. There was a line halfway around the building with guests waiting to get in. Farrell's was a popular place to celebrate special events: birthdays, anniversaries, teenage gatherings. Just as Mr. Farrell began to speak, one of the servers, a young lady, yelled out.

"Ladies and gentlemen, may I have your attention, please. Over here, we have Alex, and Alex came in to celebrate his ninth birthday." She grabbed Alex and helped him stand on a chair. He stood there, beaming from ear to ear with pride, as he looked around at the crowd at Farrell's.

"On the beat of the drum, I want you to all join me and sing Alex the happy birthday song."

The drum beat, and the crowd began to sing.

At this point, Mr. Farrell whispered in my ear, "David, what kind of business are we in?" I thought for a moment, and then responded with my answer. "Why, we're in the ice cream business," I said.

"No," Mr. Farrell said. "Look at Alex. Look at his parents, his grandparents, and the rest of his family. Look at the pride in his eyes. What kind of business are we in?"

I paused, noticing the signs of joy on all their faces, and responded, "Are we in the memory business?"

He replied quickly, "You've got it, son. Now come with me."

Back to the dish room we went. Now Mr. Farrell removed his coat and handed it to the store manager to hold. He held up a plate in one hand and a glass in the other, and said, "David, if this plate gets out in front of Alex's family with this dried piece of lettuce on it, and this glass with smeared lipstick gets in front of Alex's mom, what kind of memory will they have?"

I shook my head, embarrassed, and said, "A bad one, sir."

"That's right. Your job has a purpose, an important purpose. You protect the families' memories that we want to create, that will last a lifetime."

Mr. Farrell did something very strange. He glanced over at the store manager, Mr. Beam, for just a moment. Then he rolled up his sleeves, and said, "Now, let me show you how to do your job, and do it properly." Mr. Farrell was impacting both me and the store manager, instructing us as to our individual purposes in delivering the guest experience.

"Tomorrow morning—at 7:30 sharp—we're going to have an all-store meeting," Mr. Farrell said. "David, I look forward to seeing you there."

I quietly thought to myself, "An early morning meeting, and on a Saturday?" That was my only day off. It was my personal time to catch up on my sleep. I felt myself reluctantly smiling and replying to Mr. Farrell, "I look forward to it."

The next morning at 7:30 am, I arrived and headed to the back of the room to find an open seat. Mr. Farrell stood up, enthusiastically, with the store manager, Dennis Beam, standing by his side.

"Everybody, please stand," he said.

We all stood, and looked around at each other, wondering, "What the heck is going on?"

Mr. Farrell continued. "Now together, let's hear it."

"Hear what?" We thought, as we just looked around at each other, not a little lost, a lot lost. "Come on. Give me the Farrell's *Purpose* statement, out loud, and with enthusiasm," he said, with pride.

No one answered. We couldn't because we didn't know the purpose statement. We had never heard of it. Mr. Farrell looked over at Mr. Beam again, and a subtle glare came across his face. Mr. Farrell continued. "No problem," he said. "Me and Dennis will lead you."

Then, with the biggest smile and enthusiastic fashion, he began. "Farrell's features fabulous food and fantastic fountain fantasies for frolicking, fun-filled, festive families." We looked in awe. What the heck? We hadn't heard that before.

Then he reached over to the easel next to him, flipped the page, and said, "Now, come on, let's say it together, with enthusiasm. Come on, let me see what you've got."

We recited the Farrell's themed *Purpose* statement. He looked back and said, "Louder, and with more enthusiasm." We did it again. "One more time," and we did it again.

Now, Mr. Farrell's voice lowered. "I do not want this restaurant to open again without you getting in a circle and chanting our *Purpose* statement three times, with enthusiasm."

It was like the scene in the dish room the day before. Mr. Farrell was the champion of the Farrell's theme. It was his job to seed our subconscious minds with the Farrell's themed *Purpose* statement so we could make it a reality with every guest we served. Mr. Farrell was setting us up for success, and by doing so, was setting up the Farrell's experience for success.

He ended the meeting by saying, "Now, everyone who visits our restaurant must be greeted with a smile, so they leave with a smile, and a little dose of happy-itis. Our guests might forget what you say and do, but they will never forget how you make them feel. We are in the memory-building business. Everybody's going to remember their family visit at Farrell's Ice Cream Parlour Restaurant."

Then he said, "It's up to each of you to deliver your individual job duties with enthusiasm, so every guest that enters our doors leaves feeling the Farrell's experience. Each of you has the most important job at Farrell's Ice Cream Parlour Restaurant. Thank you very much."

Everybody started to leave, but I waited. I waited until every single person disappeared. Then I walked up to Mr. Farrell.

"Sir, may I ask you a question?" I asked.

He replied, "Yes, young man."

"How does it feel to know what you want?"

He smiled and said, "David, it's glorious because nothing starts until you know what you want. I'm glad you asked this question. Wait for a minute. I'll be right back," and off he ran to his car.

He came back with a book, and he handed it to me, and said, "You read this book three times. Highlight everything that you'd like to discuss with me, whether it

TAKEAWAYS

Mr. Farrell was the champion of the Farrell's theme. It was his job to seed our subconscious minds with the Farrell's themed *Purpose* statement so we could make it a reality with every guest we served.

> **"Our guests might forget what you say and do, but they will never forget how you make them feel."**

makes sense or not. If you're willing to do that, I'm willing to be your mentor. I visit my restaurant here in Sacramento every other month, and when I do so, I'll carve out one hour for you. I will become your personal mentor, for as long as you study this work and become a disciple of it—but there will be a price to pay, and when I see you've learned the work and executed the principles, I'm going to share with you what you'll owe me."

The book was *Think and Grow Rich*, by Dr. Napoleon Hill. I quickly saw that the principles in this book had the power to change lives—my life.

Mr. Farrell became my mentor. Under his guidance, I began to understand Dr. Hill's *Science of Success* philosophy lessons and how they fit into developing one's *Life Purpose*. It was the beginning of my *Live Ready*® experience.

Farrell's Ice Cream Parlour Restaurant's beginning *Purpose* was good food and great ice cream desserts, but that wasn't enough to attract a high level of success. When Mr. Farrell found his Big Idea—celebrations, birthdays, anniversaries, creating memories to last a lifetime—and connected it to his *Purpose*, then the Farrells' experience was born, and the guests came.

Napoleon Hill introduced the concept of Big Ideas. He explained that when you find your Big Idea and connect it to your *Purpose*, theming it so each associate understands it, then they can execute the actions needed to create the guest feeling that validates the *Purpose*.

Everyone needs a strong, definite *Purpose* to work toward. A *Purpose* is what gives meaning to life. It's the power that drives high end achievement.

Mr. Farrell understood this, and he knew how to put all the success principles behind his *Life Purpose* to work. When he taught the Big Idea of his *Life Purpose* to the employees at the Farrell's Sacramento location, he was building our character. He fired up our imaginations, so we gained the *Personal Initiative, Controlled Enthusiasm,* and *Self-Discipline* we needed to concentrate our efforts and perform our individual duties with excellence.

As we recited the Farrell's themed *Purpose* statement every day, we became invested in it. Our work environment improved, our morale improved, and the guest experience became excellent.

At first glance, the beautiful family memories created at Farrell's appear to be a side effect of the way the restaurant was run—not the *Purpose* behind it—but Mr. Farrell designed his business this way. It was his specialization, his niche Big Idea that set him apart and attracted the customer base he wanted. Once we understood that *Purpose* and were invested in it, we were committed to doing everything we could to provide the Farrell's experience.

This impacted me on a personal level, too. I specialized in being the best dishwasher I could be to deliver the Farrell's themed *Purpose*. I was on board, enthusiastic, and inspired.

With a unified and enthusiastic team of associates in all the Farrells' locations, Mr. Farrell was free to budget his money and time in ways that enhanced the customer experience, such as providing real China plates and real silverware to create a dining experience that would be unforgettable. Likewise, I budgeted my time to study and to attend my classes at the college. When I was at work, I budgeted my time in ways that made me both efficient and effective. I learned the valuable lesson of *Time Blocking* to get what you want.

That's when I started seeing opportunities for me to make a difference. By embracing the Farrell's themed *Purpose*, it became part of *who I was*, and I quickly moved up within the company. When the opportunity to become an assistant manager presented

TAKEAWAYS

Everyone needs a strong, definite *Purpose* to work toward. A *Purpose* is what gives meaning to life. It's the power that drives high end achievement.

> **One beautiful advantage of having a themed *Life Purpose* is that it inspires the cooperation of others.**

itself, I made that choice quickly and firmly, and I never looked back.

One beautiful advantage of having a themed *Life Purpose* is that it inspires the cooperation of others, the same way that Mr. Farrell inspired me and the rest of the associates at the Farrell's locations throughout the entire country. That cooperation and enthusiasm propelled me forward from one position to the next and then the next. I will always be thankful for Mr. Farrell's guidance.

A final—but most important—advantage of embracing a sense of *Purpose* is that it builds success consciousness. *Pure Non-Drifters* are aware of their past achievements, their current successes, and their future victories. It becomes a habit to expect triumph—and this is what the *Live Ready*® concept is all about.

Looking back, I'm sure that's how Mr. Farrell saw me when he offered to become my mentor. At that point, the success of his ice cream parlour restaurant was wrapped up in my success as a dishwasher and every other employee's success in their individual positions. He gave me a *Purpose* I could understand and embrace in my dishwasher position—and then he gave me another *Purpose*: to become a disciple of Napoleon Hill's work and use his principles to change my life.

It was a direct answer to my earnest question: "What does it feel like to know what you want?" Mr. Farrell taught me that knowing what you want creates a sense of *Purpose*—your *Life Purpose*. It provides a theme that carries your message forward to the world.

One thing that Mr. Farrell understood very well was that he had to find his Big Idea and theme it into his *Business Purpose* to succeed. He traveled to every Farrell's restaurant to ensure all associates,

Beyond Think and Grow Rich

in every location, understood what the Farrell's themed *Purpose* was and what his Big Idea was. We needed the themed *Purpose* to guide us. At the same time, we had to be motivated to embrace that *Purpose* as if it was our very own.

Motivation shows up in different ways for different people. Some associates of Farrell's just wanted a job. If they could not become believers of the Farrell's themed *Purpose*, in most cases they simply gained the motivation to leave on their own, or they were motivated to accept that Farrell's was not the place for them.

Most, like myself, loved our job roles once we understood the *Purpose*: we were in the business of creating happy-itis.

Love is the greatest motivator. Farrell's Ice Cream Parlour Restaurants was a labor of love for Mr. Farrell and a character-building experience for most of the young men and women that worked there.

Once Mr. Farrell introduced me to *Think and Grow Rich* by Dr. Napoleon Hill, and I became a disciple of his work, I was able to develop my own *Life Purpose* and grow out of the circumstances I started life with. When I was 28 years old, I moved back to Salt Lake City and became Farrell's youngest franchise owner. I moved back with a different belief than the one I started life with. I learned that success was meant for me, and that I had the power to help change the beliefs of others. I had gained a *Life Purpose* and the motivation to achieve it.

During this period, Mr. Farrell reminded me that I still owed him the payment for his mentoring services and that it was now time for me to repay him. He explained that I could not truly become a disciple of these success principles until I become a teacher of them. Therefore, he asked me to join him in giving the gift of my time in the service of others, in what he called the payment of "Time Tithing."

Through the gift of "Time Tithing" I mastered the Think and Grow Rich principles and taught them to thousands of students. Mr. Farrell was correct; it was through this process I truly became a disciple of them.

In the beginning, I didn't know what I was going to do with my life. Now, I own several successful companies. I've dedicated myself to being a disciple of Napoleon Hill's work and other *Success Mindset* philosophies. That means I'm constantly working on Big Ideas on a personal level as well as a professional one, *Living Ready* for the challenge of continual development.

In the beginning, it meant reading *Think and Grow Rich*—taking lots of notes and asking Mr. Farrell lots of questions—and turning Big Ideas into actions.

Here's the thing. It's possible to choose a purpose and start executing the action to achieve it, and then get distracted. Remembering to be the *Switch Master of Your Own Thought*® and *Pivot to Positive*® will be required over and over again, until you build the *Habit of Success* to gain what you want.

This is as evident in business as it is in personal life. Enormous changes in our economy have hinged on the ability of a few non-drifter leaders to choose the *Life Purpose* they embraced and then hold it firmly in their minds until they achieved it.

Take, for instance, Jeff Bezos, a computational-minded individual. He had what he thought was his Big Idea with the purpose of starting an online bookstore. In the beginning, he stored books in his garage, and oftentimes he delivered them to city residents himself. Before long, he realized he was tired, working long hours, and not making the money needed to survive. He knew there had to be a better Big Idea for his business model.

While most other innovators were looking at what was going to change over the next decade and how they could fill a new need, Jeff Bezos did the opposite: he looked for market needs he believed would NOT change over the next ten years. His Big Idea was to identify these stable market needs and build a superior online delivery system for those needs.

Bezos and a fellow Amazon engineer decided to add a new Big Idea to the Amazon *Purpose*, a newly developed software program for the online bookstore. Just 30 days after its completion, Bezos and his Amazon associate were selling and delivering books throughout the United States and 45 countries.

WOW.

Jeff Bezos merged the idea of an online bookstore with the Big Idea of an effective delivery system. He created an offering of cost-effective products with a quick delivery service and provided a better customer experience, and it worked.

But Bezos still didn't earn a return on his investment.

As discouraging as that must have been, Bezos kept a *Positive-State-of-Mind*. He refocused his thoughts and actions. He knew he was going to be successful, and he kept working on strengthening the Amazon themed purpose with each new Big Idea he discovered along the way.

As he began to work on the software more and more, he realized that books weren't the only items that would remain consistent over a decade. Electronics fit the category and toys fit that category as well. He expanded the Amazon themed *Purpose* and began selling more and more products.

When Jeff Bezos first started his journey, he was asked in an interview, "What do you do?"

He very humbly said, "I sell books online."

Ten years later, he was asked, "What do you do, Mr. Bezos?" At that point, Jeff Bezos didn't even look like the same guy. Now he was standing up straight, he was fit, and he was well dressed.

Bezos answered, "I sell merchandise online."

"What kind of merchandise do you sell?"

"Whatever I want."

His confidence had grown, and so had his themed *Purpose*. Now he had many more Big Ideas incorporated into the Amazon *Purpose*, themed in such a way that his associates, guests, and customers easily saw what the Amazon themed *Purpose* delivered. Amazon began to dominate the retail market.

Within a short time, Amazon became the prominent delivery system for anything retailed. Finally, Amazon started making money—a lot of money.

Jeff Bezos had moved from the idea of an online bookstore to the Big Idea of selling anything that could be sold online, revolutionizing retail.

In essence, he said, "I will sell anything that's sellable online." And while he didn't say, "I'll eliminate brick-and-mortar retail stores," he became their number one competitor.

Amazon started out simple and remained simple, selling anything that could be sold online, challenging the brick-and-mortar sales experience, and Jeff Bezos became the wealthiest person in the world.

What a wonderful success story, right?

It is, but there is much more to this story.

Jeff Bezos was the valedictorian of his high school. When he graduated, he gave a speech that shared his *Life Purpose* and personal Big Idea.

Here's the thing. Amazon was his *Business Purpose*, not his *Life Purpose*.

His *Life Purpose* was to one day travel into space.

Jeff Bezos consistently told his brother, "One day, Mark, we will travel into outer space. We will build our own spaceship and go into outer space. Just you wait and see."

Amazon became the Big Idea that enabled Jeff Bezos to accomplish his *Life Purpose* Big Idea: Space travel.

On Tuesday, July 20, 2021, Jeff Bezos blasted off on his spaceship, the Blue Origin NS-16. His crew consisted of his brother, Mark, along with an 18-year-old physics student, Oliver Daemon, and an 82-year-old woman aviator named Wally Funk.

Wally Funk was one of 13 women who trained with the privately funded Women in Space Program in the 1960s. Funk was fully trained, but the program was canceled, and none of the women experienced space travel. When Jeff Bezos fulfilled his life purpose, he also helped Wally Funk accomplish hers.

At the age of 82, she became the oldest individual in history to travel in space, and Oliver Daemon the youngest. The flight lasted 10 minutes and reached an ultimate height of 66.5 miles, passing the internationally recognized boundary of space known as the Karman line. This exceeded the height of Virgin Galactic and Richard Branson's SpaceShipTwo flight, which happened two weeks previously, by more than 16 miles. In this dynamic journey, the Blue Origin and her crew set ALL kinds of records.

It was all due to Amazon, Jeff Bezos' Big Idea. He and his brother were able to use the personal money they earned from Amazon to fund the development of their space program, and to fulfill his *Life Purpose*, which he articulated as an 18-year-old in a valedictorian speech.

That is the life journey of a 3% *Pure Non-Drifter* visionary.

The combination of a Big Idea, *Purpose*, and *Faith-Based Action* is always the driving force behind success in business and the success of an individual.

Mr. Farrell themed his Big Idea into his *Business Purpose* statement. When he combined it with the actions that taught me how to do my many Farrell's job roles with *Purpose* and followed up with mentoring, both our lives changed for the better.

Jeff Bezos had two *Purposes*—a *Business Purpose* and a *Life Purpose*. He combined both *Purposes* with consistent, daily action that sometimes included re-thinking the way he themed his business. Now, Amazon is the largest retailer in the world. Jeff Bezos is one of the richest men in the world, and he has finally achieved space travel.

Every successful visionary knows that a focused, themed *Purpose* with actions creates an unstoppable momentum. Triumph becomes inevitable. Some people would say this is the *Law of Attraction* where like attracts like.

The process of becoming what you want to be—and then achieving it—is a day-by-day, step-by-step endeavor. It involves creating your own Big Ideas, theming them into your business or life *Purpose*, and then putting them to work for you.

Every workable personal or professional Big Idea must be based on a strong sense of *Purpose*. The *Purpose* is always the end goal, while the Big Idea becomes the vehicle that non-drifters travel in to get there.

You are the only person who can decide what you want from life, or what your purpose will be.

TAKEAWAYS

The combination of a **Big Idea, Purpose,** and **Faith-Based Action** is always the driving force behind success in business and the success of an individual.

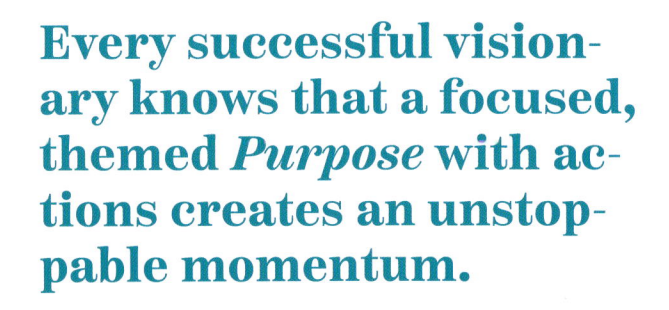

Every successful visionary knows that a focused, themed *Purpose* with actions creates an unstoppable momentum.

So, where do you start? —Take inventory.

As you go about your day, write down what you don't like on red colored sticky notes, and what you do like on green colored sticky notes. Fill a box full of each kind. After you have gathered a great deal of sticky notes, I suggest you organize them on a whiteboard or poster board, under the labels of 'like' and 'dislike.' I would recommend you set up subcategories like family/friends, faith, community, health and wealth. Then, stand back and look at them, and further organize them under these groups. You will quickly see your *Purpose* develop. This is a powerful way to learn what you want, and remember—nothing starts until you know what you want.

Summary:

Purpose is the starting point of all achievement. Nothing happens until you know what you want. The game of life cannot be won without goals and objectives that lead you to discovering your *Life's Purpose*. Most people live their lives without a *Life Purpose;* therefore, they never get what they could and should have.

If you're not clear about what you want in life, start by focusing on small goals and work toward bigger ones. Take inventory of the things that bring you satisfaction and joy in life and the things that don't. You will never be happy in a job doing the things you don't like. Find your labor of love, and that journey will lead you to your *Life Purpose* and the ability to *Live Ready*®.

Purpose *challenge*

Access QR code or at eleadertech.com/PC

"Two or more people actively engaged in the pursuit of a definite purpose with a positive mental attitude, constitute an unbeatable force."

—NAPOLEON HILL

CHAPTER THREE

Specialized Talent Team

TO OBTAIN ANY GOAL IN LIFE, YOU NEED A PROCESS—one that often begins with identifying timelines, measurables and resources to achieve what you want.

While we often intuitively think through resources, we miss an equally important step—no one person can achieve what they want in life alone. The world's most successful people have surrounded themselves with a *Specialized Talent Team* who are committed, talented and devoted to *helping them achieve their vision*.

Pure Non-Drifters understand each of these components very well. So why do most talented hardworking people fail to reach their full potential? They simply do not embrace the good news: You can't do it alone and you don't have to!

To achieve what you want, you must have a vision so strong and inspiring that others will want to achieve it just as much as you do. They need to be excited about joining your team. First, determine what skills, resources, and talents you have, and which ones you don't. Remember, you do not possess all the *Specialized Talent* needed to achieve your goals all on your own.

Developing a *Specialized Talent Team* is essential to achieving success. It allows you access to all the talent, skills, and knowledge necessary to achieve whatever it is that you want in life.

Specialized Talent Teams, while in a state of harmonious teamwork, form the hub, or the axis, of *Living Ready*. Without them, everything is simply a hope or a dream.

There's a word in the English language that's often misunderstood: That word is ignorance. Being ignorant in any one subject simply means you lack knowledge in that area. It's not a bad thing. We all have areas of ignorance, and we all have areas of *Specialized Talents*. The secret of success is knowing the difference.

Pure Non-Drifters understand this, and that's why they don't remain ignorant for long and why they achieve extraordinary results. They know when to lead, and they know when to follow. Most *Drifters* do not understand or accept this success concept. This causes them to settle for ordinary or mediocre results.

A *Drifter's* unhealthy ego is responsible for the belief that every decision must flow through them. This belief prevents the attainment of the *Rhythm of Success* and ultimately, the *Habit of Success*.

It is incredibly important that you get this right. Begin by understanding and acknowledging your own talent. Remember, you must understand and acknowledge what talents you DO NOT have—and how to find those talents in others to achieve what you want.

To put this principle to work, you must take inventory of your own skills, knowledge, and *Specialized Talent*.

Remember the whiteboard exercise that you used at the end of Chapter Two to discover your *Purpose*. You can use the same process to determine what your talents are and what they are not. Write down every talent you know you possess on a green sticky note. On a red sticky note, write down every talent that you feel you lack, but you know will be necessary for you to

TAKEAWAYS

Specialized Talent Teams, while in a state of harmonious teamwork, form the hub, or the axis, of *Living Ready*. Without them, everything is simply a hope or a dream.

Genius is rarely found in one mind alone. But it is often found in the work performed by a **Specialized Talent Team**, working together as one mastermind.

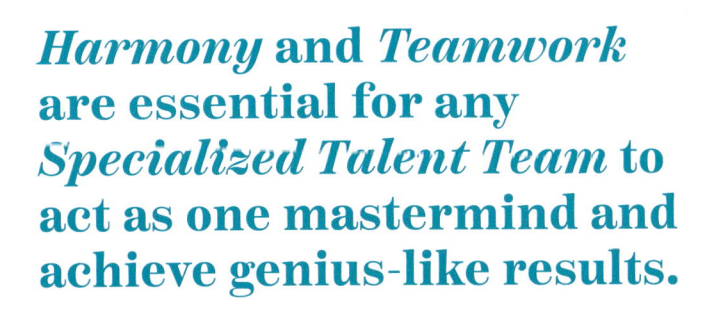

> **Harmony and Teamwork are essential for any Specialized Talent Team to act as one mastermind and achieve genius-like results.**

achieve what you want in life. Now, organize them on a whiteboard.

As you analyze your results, give attention to all the specialized talent that you will need to achieve what you want. Give extra attention to the talents you do not personally possess. Now, ask yourself, "Who do I know who has mastered the talents I lack?" These are the potential members you should invite to join your *Specialized Talent Team*. This mastermind team will help you achieve your goals, objectives, or *Life Purpose*.

Combining two or more minds together to work in complete *Harmony* and *Teamwork* creates *Thought-Power*. Genius is rarely found in one mind alone. But it is often found in the work performed by a *Specialized Talent Team*, working together as one mastermind.

Harmony and *Teamwork* are essential for any *Specialized Talent Team* to act as one mastermind and achieve genius-like results. This requires all members to serve while in a *Positive-State-of-Mind*. To achieve a team-positive mindset, every member must understand and embrace the goals, objectives, or *Purpose*. They must acknowledge which individual talent they are contributing and be willing to enthusiastically offer their talent to successfully accomplish their common ambition. Team members operating in a *Positive-State-of-Mind* treat each other with respect. When each team member is *Purpose*-driven and serves with a *Pleasing Personality*, group *Harmony* and *Teamwork* are achieved. And this is where the team's *Thought-Power* moves into the *Genius Zone*.

We have discussed why only 30% of businesses survive past their first ten years. The reasons behind the failure rate extend beyond a lack of purpose or a business-negative mindset. Often the leaders of businesses that fail haven't determined the skills they need to succeed; therefore, they haven't created a *Specialized Talent Team* to compensate for talents that were lacking. One cannot obtain great *Thought-Power* without the utilization of a *Specialized Talent Team*.

Extraordinary results can only be achieved through shared *Talent* and *Teamwork*. That is the secret of how great fortunes, great successes, and great relationships are achieved. This *Live Ready*® principle requires every brain to become a broadcasting system and a receiving station for the vibration of thought, causing ideas to flash into your mind. More importantly, when you become a broadcasting and receiving system, you are enabled to look for outstanding ideas and accept them, so you don't reject the nudge of *Thought-Power*.

Britnie Turner's story is a wonderful example of how to use the *Specialized Talent Team* to get what you could and should have in life.

Every successful *Pure Non-Drifter*, like Britnie, has a strong, clear vision of what they want. This drives their passion and lays the groundwork for their *Life Purpose*.

Britnie Turner's *Purpose* came to her as a dream in the night, when she was just twelve years old. As a home-schooled farm girl in South Carolina, USA, Britnie developed a love for people, for animals, and for God, and that love helped create her *Life Purpose*. In Britnie's reoccurring dream, she saw herself as a missionary in Africa. That dream ignited a spark and set her on a path that would change thousands of lives in some of the most impoverished communities across the world. It became a vision that guided Britnie's day-to-day life.

In ninth grade, Britnie began attending a local high school. She made her own kind of 'cool' by inviting her friends to join her first *Specialized Talent Team* to work with her on the weekends, having fun by cleaning up the yards of elderly people in her community.

But this effort just wasn't enough. Britnie craved the missions she dreamed about. From the time she was 13 years old, she worked multiple jobs at once, even during the school year. She saved that money to pay for yearly trips to third-world countries, where she had a chance to see first-hand the difficulties people living in other cultures and nations experienced.

When she wasn't traveling, at school, or participating in service projects in her community, Britnie studied missionary leadership. One of the classes she took required her to write her own eulogy—an exercise that she says is one of the most clarifying things a person can do when they want to define their *Life Purpose*.

She wrote it out, and it changed her life forever.

In 2007, at the age of 18, Britnie led a team of friends to Central America. This was one of the most harrowing and influential experiences of her life.

The mission centered around the development of a woman's conference. At the end of the conference, she and other missionaries were praying over people and talking with those that attended. One of the very last people that Britnie spoke to was a little girl around the age of eight. She asked the girl her name, so she could pray with her, but the translator said the girl couldn't speak. Britnie learned that when the girl was an infant, her father had abused her. In the process, he destroyed her vocal cords. Britnie was distraught. When she looked into the eyes of this little girl she saw dark hopelessness. She felt this little girl would possibly never escape the nightmare she suffered. Britnie knew she must personally get involved to help this little girl and other children like her.

Anger, frustration, and sadness tormented Britnie's thoughts. In this impoverished region, child abuse was far too common, and sometimes it resulted in the death of a child. Britnie went back to her tent, distressed. She fell to her knees and prayed. At that moment, she didn't care about the difficulties in front of her. She just wanted to find a way to stop this unacceptable child abuse, and she was willing to do whatever she had to do, to be part of the solution.

That moment of prayer was a turning point in Britnie's life. During her return travels, she felt her subconscious mind become a receiver for *Infinite Intelligence*. Britnie heard God's directions loud and clear—she was directed to stop her missionary work and redirect her efforts to business.

She hated the idea.

At that time in her life, Britnie believed big business was evil. She was anti corporate greed and money. Accepting God's will for her meant that she had to readjust the seeding of her subconscious, which was that big corporations were bad, that money was evil. She had to accept that she needed the help of caring businesses to achieve her desired end results.

With the image of that little girl burned into her mind, Britnie realized that money is a resource that can be used for good, a gift that can be used for the development of others, including re-inventing nations. She began to understand that money makes a good person better, because of the impact it can create, and money makes a bad person worse, because their arrogance is magnified.

Her perspective changed. Britnie learned that money can be an expansion tool of the heart, and that wealth is a resource for getting things done. One can do well and do good at the same time.

After she returned from Central America, Britnie took another leadership class. The teacher presented an idea that Britnie latched onto immediately: if she bought a house and rented rooms out, she could make more money than she owed for her mortgage payment.

This thought sank into Britnie's mind, and she developed her first Big Idea: She was going to create wealth through real estate, to enable her to become a change-maker in third world countries.

In 2007, at just the age of 18, she bought her first house. The real estate agent she worked with introduced her to the idea of house-flipping. Britnie was inspired and determined to become an expert in creating wealth through real estate, to achieve her *Life Purpose*.

To gain the specialized knowledge she needed, Britnie realized she would have to embark on a non-traditional educational path, which was not offered in college. She would need to find experts in the house-flipping industry to teach her what she needed to know.

Around this time, another opportunity was presented to her in the form of a book:

TAKEAWAYS

Money makes a good person better, because of the impact it can create, and **money makes a bad person worse**, because their arrogance is magnified.

> **Money can be an expansion tool of the heart, and that wealth is a resource for getting things done.**

Think and Grow Rich, by Dr. Napoleon Hill. While it was written in 1937 English, the message was clear. It taught her how to achieve her *Life Purpose* by finding the seed of opportunity in every crisis, keeping a *Positive-State-of-Mind,* and creating *Specialized Talent Teams*. This book set her brain on fire with positive thoughts.

With the principles of *Think and Grow Rich* in her heart and the need to learn more about real estate in her head, Britnie did something unconventional. She moved to Nashville, Tennessee, USA to work for someone who could teach her the real estate business. It was the first of many experiences in which Britnie became a devoted team member, just so she could develop her own *Specialized Talents* and skills and gain the knowledge she was looking for.

Sixty days into her first real estate job, Britnie was fired. While she was disappointed, she wasn't deterred. Britnie quickly found a way to *Pivot to Positive*®. She found another company and offered to work for them, free of charge, just to learn the real estate business.

This commitment left Britnie with limited cash, which required her to live in her car for nine months. She still had a house payment and other bills. She survived on odd jobs and small commissions, which she made by finding renters for properties that other people in the business couldn't seem to rent out. Her focus remained on learning.

And she did learn. She started by doing paperwork, *Going the Extra Mile* to make herself valuable to the people she worked for, and drawing on their expertise along the way. She took notes of everything that happened around her. Where she saw gaps and needs not being filled, she went the *Extra Mile* to find ways to fill them. In the process, she learned how to find projects, how to make

Beyond Think and Grow Rich

deals, how to get the best subcontractors, how to design the projects, and how to find funding.

Her education was a win-win situation. Britnie was able to draw on the experience, training, and specialized knowledge of others. She modeled her work after theirs. While she learned, they had the advantage of her contribution of bringing money into their company—and they didn't have to pay her a cent. Britnie's gift of service enabled her to receive their knowledge in return. Without them even knowing it, Britnie had developed them into her second *Specialized Talent Team*.

She quickly concluded that there were limitless opportunities for people who create value.

Britnie's goal was to become financially set by the time she was 26 years old, so she could build an orphanage in Africa. In 2009, at the age of 20, Britnie opened her first business, and called it the Aerial Development Group.

She assembled an eclectic group as her *Specialized Talent Team* to find opportunities and act upon them. During those first few years, Britnie managed rental portfolios, worked as a real estate agent, and remodeled homes. She found her *Rhythm of Success*. Britnie used her resources and contacts to buy an owner-financed property. She then used her friend's credit card to pay for repairs and subcontracting crews.

The night before the sale of the house to a new owner closed, it was robbed. All the copper wiring and every appliance, except the refrigerator, were taken. Closing was delayed for three months while Britnie made the repairs and pulled the deal back together. When the deal finally closed, she made her first real estate profit of $40,000.

Britnie was now officially in the house-flipping business.

That was just the beginning of the Aerial Development Group's success.

From the start, Britnie made her *Business Purpose* clear: to empower people, to sustain the planet, and to utilize the power of capitalism for good. This powerful mission statement themed her Big Idea—using real estate profits to enact positive change worldwide. She always intended to elevate lives and communities around the world. That mission was executed brilliantly at the Aerial Development Group, and in all the *Specialized Talent Teams* she created and drew upon in order to achieve her *Company Purpose*.

Since the opening of the Aerial Development Group, Britnie has launched several other companies under the Aerial name, providing partnerships that create value on several fronts. This includes Aerial Recovery, which provides disaster aid, and a media production company called Aerial Productions.

Aerial Productions was launched with the intention of showing people in impoverished areas a better vision of what their lives could and should be. Britnie wanted this media business to create hope for people like the little girl she met in Central America, and children like her around the world, so they could understand they matter, and that they have great worth as children of God.

This business, like all her other businesses, depended on *Specialized Talent Teams*. The team members from each company worked together enthusiastically and harmoniously to achieve the *Business Purpose* and help Britnie reach her *Life Purpose*—using real estate profits to enact positive change worldwide.

As Aerial expanded, Britnie was able to fulfill her vision of building an orphanage, which she quickly noticed created some interesting financial reactions. She realized that the real estate development of the orphanage property created an economic hot spot. This provided a series of job opportunities for the area where families were so impoverished, improving the lives of everyone involved. Britnie reaffirmed her belief that positive and good can overcome negative and evil. She had discovered the formula to combat evil—economic empowerment.

Families gained the power of positive choice, which replaced the horrendous negative evil choices that are far too common in impoverished regions around the world.

During the process of developing the orphanage, other businesses bought the land around it. Britnie began to understand that if you can share the vision of potential, the economy grows. People have opportunities they have never had before. As their desperation fades, good flourishes, and evil can be stifled.

The *Specialized Talent Teams* that Britnie built and utilized during this process provided a win for everyone. That's exactly what Britnie wanted. Her objective, goal, and *Purpose* have always been focused on developing security and happiness for everyone, in every community she serves.

Through her work with Aerial and its many cooperative efforts, Britnie developed her *Formula for Success*. This formula works precisely because it relies on the development and utilization of local *Specialized Talent Teams*. And best of all, her formula can be used again and again, no matter what goal she is working on.

To obtain any goal, objective, or *Life Purpose*, you need a process that ensures success. This begins with identifying the necessary resources, timelines, and measurable steps to achieve your desired end-result. So, why do so many people fail to achieve what they want? They don't embrace the obvious—you can't do it alone.

Before I finish sharing Britnie's story, let me share a few fundamental rules of a *Specialized Talent Team:*

Get clear about what you want: Examine what you want to achieve until you know the difference between the facts and opinions. Only then can you develop a goal, objective, or *Life Purpose* with the power of a clear vision behind it.

Supercharge your Talent: Once you're clear about your *Purpose,* multiply your talent, skills, and knowledge by creating *Specialized Talent Teams*. This increases the possibility of entering the *Genius Zone*—the sweet spot where your strategies are clear, and your execution level is high.

Develop deep connections: The *Rhythm of Success* is best achieved when team members respect each other enough to work together long-term, building a *Habit of Success* culture where everyone achieves their goals, objectives, and *Purposes*. The goal of *Specialized Talent Teams* is to create greater opportunities for everyone involved.

Positive-State-of-Mind: This *Success Mindset* is more than a well-worn platitude. Positive thinking empowers you to look for the good in your daily circumstances, your team members, and your own efforts. When you stay positive, you're able to notice more opportunities and find solutions to any adversity that tries to prevent you from getting what you want. Be careful of what you think because you will get it—good or bad!

Britnie Turner lives these success concepts, and her *Specialized Talent Teams* reflect it. Her 'Formula for Success' starts with a clear vision of what she wants to accomplish. Then she determines what specialized talent is required to accomplish her goals, objectives, or *Life Purpose*, and, most importantly, where to find the talent needed to achieve her desired end-results.

By the time Britnie was flipping houses, she was already becoming an expert in developing and utilizing *Specialized Talent Teams*. What started out with a team of subcontractors and funding sources for flipping houses provided her with the expertise she needed to extend the reach of her companies, so she could provide humanitarian aid and economic growth worldwide. Britnie developed *Personal Initiative* and *Self-Discipline* to plan, organize, execute, and follow through to get what she wanted. She emphasized the importance of maintaining a *Success Mindset*, so her teams could work together in complete *Harmony* and *Teamwork*.

These teams now work in selected areas around the world to provide necessities like clean water, power, and infrastructure. Britnie can often be found at disaster scenes, where she directs her *Specialized Talent Teams* to provide food, medicines, and other resources. Once relief is provided, she focuses on helping make the local communities more successful and economically stable, while retaining their cultural roots.

Once again, Britnie uses *Specialized Talent Teams* to partner with other relief groups, local business leaders, and governments, to address the root causes behind larger social issues. All team members are taught to work in harmony on their common objectives, the same way that her *Specialized Talent Teams* work in harmony to flip houses. When they're all working in *Harmony* and *Teamwork*, everyone wins. Economies are stabilized, and that trickles down to the people who need it most—the orphans, the abused children, and families that were once torn apart by poverty and inhumane choices.

Britnie developed the G-Force Leadership Retreat to teach her 'Formula for Success', and how to develop *Specialized Talent Teams*. She holds her retreat at a resort she built and owns in the Virgin Islands.

But like so many of Britnie's blessings, this great accomplishment did not come without obstacles and temporary defeats.

The week before her scheduled grand opening, a hurricane hit the Virgin Islands, and hit them hard! Britnie's island resort was completely destroyed. While most people would have given up—thinking it was not meant to be—Britnie has no giving up in her heart or soul. She maintained a *Positive-State-of-Mind*, starting with the development of a new *Specialized Talent Team*, working in *Harmony* to rebuild her dream leadership resort stronger and better. The first two members of that team were her mom and dad.

Britnie and her parents went back to the island, and they rebuilt the resort. This is a perfect example of how she always looks for the seed of a greater benefit in every adversity that she faces.

Today, the resort is open as a leadership get-away, where people come to learn how to develop a *Purpose*, find Big Ideas, and theme them in such a way that everybody understands exactly what you do and why you do it. Britnie is successful precisely because she understands that getting what she wants—including wide scale change—depends on the resources you have available.

Many times, the best resources are other people, working together in *Harmony* and *Teamwork* on a common *Purpose*. When you align yourself through the power of *Teamwork* with people who have the talent, skills, experience, and knowledge to get what you want,

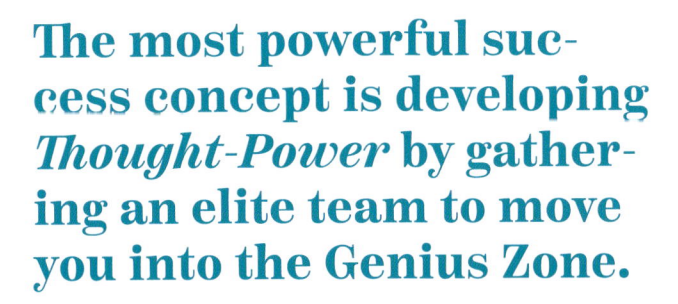

The most powerful success concept is developing *Thought-Power* by gathering an elite team to move you into the Genius Zone.

your resources expand. The likelihood that you will achieve your *Purpose* skyrockets.

No matter what you want to achieve, this model sets you up for success. You can overcome practically every obstacle when you involve others who enthusiastically apply their assets of capital and talent.

I should warn you—if done correctly, the side effect of this approach will go beyond just wealth or tangible business success; it will create a positive energy that produces remarkable success in other areas of your life.

As you think about your goals, objectives, or *Life Purpose,* embrace the idea that you may not have all the resources to get what you could and should have on your own—and you don't have to. The most powerful success concept is developing *Thought-Power* by gathering an elite team to move you into the *Genius Zone.*

Thought-Power is achieved as every team member works harmoniously and enthusiastically with other team members. Each becomes a sending and receiving station, sharing ideas almost automatically. In some cases, it will seem as if team members are reading each other's thoughts. In these situations, the tremendous momentum generated by harmonious *Teamwork* propels projects forward, and success becomes inevitable.

This is the power of developing and utilizing a *Specialized Talent Team.*

There are two things to remember as you consider who to invite to help you achieve your *Purpose.* One, a *Specialized Talent Team* is not just a group of friends. The type of collaboration you're looking for extends beyond sharing interesting ideas. It involves serious focus and attention, but more importantly, it involves resources: the talents, skills, expertise, and experience that can help you achieve what you want. As you build your team, bring in the elite team members who provide those resources best.

Second, no matter what venture you embark on, you always get what you give—so give your all. It is extremely important to create the perfect environment for harmonious *Teamwork*. By staying in a *Positive-State-of-Mind* you influence team members to do the same. As team members grow in confidence, they take the *Personal Initiative* to create value—much like Britnie did when she learned to flip houses. They engage fully in the process, and their participation becomes their passion.

When team members work together harmoniously, it's hard to imagine a problem they can't solve.

Now—make your plan to build a *Specialized Talent Team* that will best serve the achievement of your goals, objectives, or *Life Purpose*.

TAKEAWAYS

When you align yourself through the power of *Teamwork* with people who have the talent, skills, experience, and knowledge to get what you want, your resources expand. The likelihood that you will achieve your *Purpose* skyrockets.

Summary:

To obtain any goal, objective, or *Life Purpose*, first you must determine what skills, resources, and *Specialized Talents* you have, and which ones you don't. No one person possesses all the *Specialized Talent* necessary to achieve most of their goals and objectives, and certainly not their *Life Purpose*, on their own.

Developing a *Specialized Talent Team* is essential to achieve success. It allows you access to all the talent, skills, and knowledge necessary to achieve whatever it is that you want in life.

When each team member is *Purpose*-driven and serves with a *Pleasing Personality*, group *Harmony* and *Teamwork* are achieved. And this is where the team's *Thought-Power* moves into the *Genius Zone*.

Specialized Talent Team *challenge*

Access QR code or at eleadertech.com/STTC

Beyond Think and Grow Rich

"Faith is taking the first step even when you don't see the whole staircase."

—MARTIN LUTHER KING JR.

CHAPTER FOUR

Faith-Based Action

NOTHING HAPPENS UNTIL AN ACTION IS PUT INTO motion, followed by another one and another one until your goals, objectives, or *Life Purpose* are achieved.

There's a difference between an action based on faith and one that is not. Every *Faith-Based Action* will take you one step closer to achieving your goals, objectives, or *Life Purpose*.

What is faith? Faith is believing in something so deeply that you can see it and touch it—you imagine it is a done deal. Faith is trusting that every action you take will bring you closer to achieving those things you want. Faith followed by action will get you through almost anything.

Most *Pure Non-Drifters* discover their *Life Purpose* through the process of setting goals and objectives, followed by executing well defined actions to achieve them. This journey validates what they like and more importantly what they love, making it possible to develop a clear vision of their life's *Purpose*.

Drifters fail to discover their *Life Purpose* because they are not goal setters and scorekeepers. They drift through life living on hope, plans failing because few actions are ever put into motion to achieve a goal or objective. Therefore, *Drifters* never gain the *Rhythm of Success* to start their journey to discover their *Life Purpose*.

The execution of *Faith-Based Actions* is mandatory to *Live Ready*®. It's what allows you to convert what may seem like a failure into a success. By properly utilizing the *Brain Model* process and executing adjusted *Faith-Based Actions,* adversity simply becomes an adjustment opportunity. Without *Faith-Based Action,* there would be no forward movement to initiate the development of a *Specialized Talent Team.* No steps would be taken to achieve a goal, objective, or *Life Purpose,* so no achievement could occur. People who live without *Faith-Based Action* live in limbo, stuck in a world of daydreams rather than progressing, achieving, and getting what they could and should have in life.

On the other hand, people who embrace the philosophy of *Faith-Based Action* not only take steps toward achieving their goals, objectives, or *Life Purpose,* they also build the *Rhythm of Success.* Acting in faith is a method of applying the principle of positive self-talk. It embraces courage, optimism, and the will to try, even when success is not guaranteed. *Faith-Based Action* removes limitations from your mind so you can move forward to achieve what you want.

Defining faith can be a challenge. Many people see faith as an abstract idea that represents your awareness of and coordination with the laws of nature and the Universe. Others see it differently, as a solid concept that moves them from inaction to a state of positive action.

While most people understand the power of faith as it relates to religion, many do not understand the requirement of faith when it comes to achieving a goal, objective, or *Life Purpose*. Faith is the link between *Infinite Intelligence,* the reticular activating system (RAS), and *Faith-Based Action* to achieve what you want. It's the fuel that ignites when you put a plan into motion and begin taking steps to carry out that plan. It's the quiet, powerful feeling of confidence that comes while you're executing those actions. When

TAKEAWAYS

What is faith? Faith is believing in something so deeply that you can see it and touch it—you imagine it is a done deal.

Faith is trusting that every action you take will bring you closer to achieving those things you want.

you're acting in faith, you expect success, and you experience one of the most powerful positive mental states achievable.

Faith is the principle that causes you to act. It's the passion behind action that creates a burning desire to achieve a goal, objective, or *Life Purpose*.

Some develop a goal and a good plan for achieving it, but they lack faith—the driving force behind their actions—so their effort is only half-hearted. They often feel apathetic about what they want so they move lethargically. They're like a toy train set with worn-down batteries. They may start out strong, but before long, they lose power, fizzle out, and become stranded on the tracks.

People who have real faith have internal power that drives them forward, following through with the plans they make with enthusiasm and excitement. They remain in a *Positive-State-of-Mind,* imagining their actions have already achieved what they want, so that their minds are conditioned to receive inspiration through *Infinite Intelligence* or the RAS.

Because people with faith are open to all avenues to achieve their goal, objective, or *Life Purpose,* they develop a pattern of recognizing new opportunities, discovered during their success journey, and act upon them. This starts the *Rhythm of Success* and, in time, creates the *Habit of Success,* which is a continual flow of energized action to achieve what you want. The execution of *Faith-Based Action* is a requirement of success, and this act is often not natural to most people. But once you achieve the *Habit of Success,* execution becomes natural, like guiding a boat along with the current rather than paddling upstream.

You might also think of faith as an absolute refusal to give up on

> **When you're acting in faith, you focus intensely on what you want, which allows you to access your *Thought-Power* to achieve it.**

your goals, objectives, or *Life Purpose*. When you look at faith this way, it provides motivation and inspiration for solving adversity, even when it seems impossible. It's a state-of-mind where determination, desire, and positive thought become so intertwined that taking action is the most natural thing to do to achieve what you could and should have.

A true understanding of *Faith-Based Action* comes as you fully understand the *Brain Model's* inner workings and how to seed your subconscious mind with success thoughts. When you're acting in faith, you focus intensely on what you want, which allows you to access your *Thought-Power* to achieve it.

This is evident in the life of Misty Copeland. Although her early life was challenging, she focused on her goals, developed a strong *Life Purpose*, and refused to give up on her dream.

On June 30, 2015, Misty Copeland became the first African American Principal Dancer for the American Ballet Theatre, one of the top three ballet companies in the United States of America. Long before she stepped into a life of fame and success, she slept in a sleeping bag on the cramped floor of a small hotel room with her brothers and sisters, being raised by a single mother, unsure of where her next meal would come from.

Misty was resourceful and determined. Despite a non-traditional home life, she found peace and solace in moving her body in dance to cope with the stress of life. Eventually, this led her to discover her *Life Purpose*—to utilize classical ballet to make the world a better place for people of every skin color, body type, and culture.

Even though she didn't know it at first, Misty's ability to release stress through dance movement led her from surviving an unstable, chaotic life, directly into the spotlight, both as a phenomenal ballerina and as an advocate for racial equality. Her love of ballet inspired her to execute the *Faith-Based Action* steps that resulted in personal, professional, and multicultural success.

Misty's home life was challenging. From the time she was two years old, up through middle school, Misty experienced a stream of men coming in and out of her life as her mother switched partners. Throughout her childhood Misty didn't know her real father. The other men in her mother's life were often angry, unpredictable, and unstable.

By the time she was 13 years old, Misty understood uncertainty and confusion. The feeling in her home was one of constant change, with an edge of danger, as her mother periodically moved her and her five brothers and sisters to different households and living situations.

Misty's siblings were avid football fans, and the sports programs on television were the center of attention. They lived on processed foods like ramen noodles and canned vegetables. Misty often felt unsettled and out of place.

She dealt with the confusion by dancing. At first, she watched gymnastics videos and mimicked the gymnast Nadia Comăneci, until she could do her own 'floor routines' on the grass outside. She would often sneak into her mother's bedroom, where it was relatively quiet, and choreograph dances to Mariah Carey songs.

Dancing became Misty's escape. When she was choreographing a new sequence, she didn't think about her situation at home. She was in a *Positive-State-of-Mind* with good thoughts.

Misty hid her feelings of having to be constantly on guard. During her days at middle school, she was a hall monitor, and she auditioned to be the captain of the drill team. She won. After school, she attended the local Boys and Girls Club for about two hours, with her brothers and sisters, while

TAKEAWAYS

A true understanding of *Faith-Based Action* comes as you fully understand the Brain Model's inner workings and how to seed your subconscious mind with success thoughts.

Beyond Think and Grow Rich

she waited for her mom to get off work.

The drill team advisor, Liz Cantine, was impressed with Misty's natural abilities. She asked her to look into a ballet class that one of her friends taught at the San Pedro Boys and Girls Club.

For three weeks, Misty watched the class without participating. The instructor was a woman named Cynthia Bradley. Misty didn't have leotards, tights, or slippers, but Cynthia invited her to the floor anyway.

One day, Misty decided to join the class. Even though she didn't feel like she fit in, she walked onto the floor, dressed in gym shorts and socks, and she began to learn about ballet.

That first *Faith-Based Action* was a life-changing moment. Within a few short weeks, ballet became Misty's first Big Idea and her *Purpose*, which she themed her *Faith-Based Action* around, to make it become a reality.

Right from the beginning, Misty could mimic almost every movement she saw, and she had a keen ability to remember how to perform those movements. She was a prodigy. Within a short time, Cynthia invited Misty to take classes at her official ballet studio across town.

Most ballerinas begin dance lessons early, at least by the age of eight. Misty was small for her age, so it didn't show, but at thirteen, she was around five years behind most of the other students at Cynthia's studio.

That didn't matter much. Misty's natural ability, combined with her daily classes and practice, propelled her forward so rapidly that within eight weeks, she was dancing on the tips of her toes.

She was committed to the process, even though it required constant, vigorous practice that cut into her schedule and required the help of others. Liz Cantine, the drill team instructor, paid for Misty's leotards, tights, and slippers. Cynthia Bradley drove Misty to the ballet studio after school, and Misty's older sister, Erica, rode home with Misty on the bus, so she wouldn't have to be alone. When the evening trips got to be too much and Misty's mother began to complain about the arrangement, Cynthia offered to let

Misty stay with her during the week. It was an unusual arrangement, but it worked, and Misty continued learning.

By this time, Misty's love of classical ballet had grown beyond a passion. She was determined to become a professional ballerina, in spite of the serious obstacles she faced. Misty's first Big Idea expanded into her *Life Purpose*.

At the time, it seemed almost impossible. Besides her un-traditional home life, Misty was black and muscular. She didn't fit the stereotype of a typical ballerina, but she didn't let that stop her. She embraced daily practice and all the sacrifices it demanded.

During the next two years, Misty stayed with her mom and her brothers and sisters at a hotel on weekends, where she slept on the floor, and stayed with Cynthia's family during the week. In the ballet classes, she learned new steps and how to practice them in unison with other dancers. She performed ballet routines, made friends that cheered her on, and advanced so quickly that she soon began performing in the community.

Although Misty was naturally quiet and shy, her dedication and talent opened doors for her. Even as an amateur, she danced the lead role as Clare in *The Chocolate Nutcracker* and as the lead in other televised productions and dance competitions. Her willingness to work hard and to step into the spotlight brought her to the attention of large, professional ballet companies from across the nation. She won scholarships for summertime intensive ballet programs, which included moving to San Francisco one summer and New York City the next.

Misty took advantage of every resource she had, threw herself into ballet, and excelled. At the end of the San Francisco summer training, Misty was offered scholarships to attend ballet schools away from home from six out of seven professional studios. The only studio that turned her application away did so because she was black. Although this shocked her slightly, she kept her focus on her *Life Purpose* to become a principal ballerina with the American Ballet Theatre.

Then, a disaster on the home front almost cost her the chance to become a professional ballerina. The arrangement between Cynthia and Misty's mom became strained. Between her summers in San Francisco and New York City, their relationship blew up in an embarrassing and very public fight over Misty and her future. In the end, Misty went back home to live with her mother.

Although Misty was furious and humiliated, her mother enrolled her into another ballet school. Misty once again buckled down, practiced hard, and expanded her skills. This helped her with auditions, and she was able to secure her summer intensive training with the American Ballet Theatre in New York City.

This was a big step toward Misty's *Life Purpose*. She was able to meet and eventually befriend Paloma Herrera, one of her heroes, an Argentine woman who had become a Principal Dancer with the American Ballet Theatre. This was important for Misty, because at that time, she didn't know of many ballet dancers with brown skin. It was proof to Misty that if she executed her *Faith-Based Action* steps, she could achieve whatever she wanted.

As she entered the New York Ballet scene, she was emotionally supported by her mother, who had stabilized her life and was now taking good care of her family. Misty also built new friendships and made vital connections within the ballet world. Building these friendships was another *Faith-based Action* step that provided her with the resources she needed to continue to dance.

With the support of her teachers, her family, her friends, and her connections with other ballet dancers, Misty continued to progress. She joined the American Ballet Theatre as an Apprentice after she graduated from high school. At age 19, she joined the Corps de Ballet. She was, officially, a professional ballerina.

But that was just the beginning. Her world opened up. When she wasn't dancing with the American Ballet Theatre, she danced and taught dance, including touring and making music videos with the American Singer-Songwriter Prince. She met her birth father and became friends with him. She made friends with dancers from the Dance Theatre of Harlem, an all-black dance company. And then, at the age of 24, she became a Soloist with the American Ballet Theatre.

Through her years in training, Misty had come to realize that dancers with dark skin were not as welcome in the ballet world as dancers with light skin. She began pushing for changes that would make the ballet world friendlier for children of color. This was her second Big Idea, themed entirely around classical ballet. She wrote a children's book, *Bunheads,* to describe her journey as a black ballerina and to inspire young girls to believe in their dreams. She also asked for directors to tweak costumes in the Corps de Ballet, so that she didn't have to paint her face white to dance.

Her hard work, her natural talent for classical ballet, and her fierce insistence on being herself paid off. She had become a sending and receiving station for ballet in a way that unified her with other dancers, but she had also become a sending and receiving station for racial equality. This required her to embrace the courage to be, exactly and absolutely, who she was, and to act with integrity, which included portraying an unequivocal message that discrimination of any type is NOT okay.

At first, the changes were small, such as switching out a white cat costume for a brown one in the Corps de Ballet, so Misty could dance in her own skin color. The real triumph came when Kevin McKenzie, the Artistic Director for the American Ballet Theatre, told Misty she would be learning the principal role for a production called *Firebird.* Although it wasn't a guarantee that she'd get the role, learning the lead was an indication that she was being taken seriously.

Misty found out that she was officially cast as the Firebird through a Twitter announcement that she happened to see while helping the Dance Theatre of Harlem put on a workshop. She began crying, and the black ballet dancers there gathered around her to hug her, congratulate her, and cry happy tears with her. They felt as elated as she did because her triumph was also their triumph.

Her friends at the American Ballet Theatre were just as thrilled for her. A few years later, when she was officially promoted to be a Principal Dancer with the company, she was again surrounded by friends and fellow dancers, who had watched Misty's struggles, determination, and rise to the top.

The collective support of Misty's teachers, colleagues, family, and friends broadened her view of the value of a *Specialized Talent Team*, which also expanded her vision of her *Life Purpose*. She now embraces classical ballet as an evolving art, one that everyone can enjoy even if they don't fit the stereotypical profile of a ballerina. Her next *Faith-Based Action* steps were to utilize ballet to help children of every color and body shape discover their strengths and *Purpose* in life.

At about the same time that she was cast as the Firebird, Misty turned her eyes back toward her beginning at the San Pedro Boys and Girls Club. A public service advertising campaign allowed her to team up with other famous people, including Denzel Washington, Jennifer Lopez, Kerry Washington, Magic Johnson, and several other successful people who got their start at the Boys and Girls Clubs of America.

In 2012, Misty Copeland was inducted into the Boys and Girls Club Hall of Fame. Her work to create racial equality has expanded since then. She partners with both the Boys and Girls Clubs and MindLeaps to bring ballet into communities. Her expanded *Life Purpose* now is to help every person who wants to participate in ballet be able to enjoy it and contribute to it in their own individual ways, without the fear of judgment or overwhelming competition.

Her perseverance is paying off. In 2021, Misty published a book entitled 'Black Ballerinas,' which is a compilation of stories of 27 other black ballerinas. As with all her *Faith-Based Action* steps, it took dedication and time—in this case, 25 years—to gather and refine the stories. This Big Idea provides historical cases that a wide variety of children can draw on to support their own desires to train as classical ballerinas. It's become part of Misty Copeland's legacy.

One of the things that makes Misty's story so remarkable is her ability to flow from one situation to another, accessing *Infinite Intelligence* and using principles of the *Brain Model* to help her see opportunities and act on them. As a young ballerina facing incredible odds, she had the wherewithal to maintain a *Positive-State-of-Mind*. She noticed that she felt serene and powerful when she danced. When she saw opportunities and acted on them, she found ways to achieve her *Life Purpose* to become a professional ballerina.

To an observer, it might look as if Misty was led from one opportunity to another. That's exactly how *Infinite Intelligence* and the *Brain Model* work. When you have faith, you condition your mind to receive that flow of *Intelligence,* including all the ideas that come with it. You adapt the ideas and opportunities that you see to achieve your *Purpose.*

Faith is a very individual thing. As you step into the flow of *Infinite Intelligence* and build the *Habit of Success,* you feel motivated to act. You immerse your thoughts in a *Positive-State-of-Mind,* which allows you to gain belief in endless possibilities. And once you become a believer, you gain the power to take action to make it happen.

As you make plans to help you get what you could and should have in life, keep in mind that faith is the gateway to effective actions and powerful results. To keep that gateway open, you must remain in a *Positive-State-of-Mind*. This requires you to focus on the things you want, to the point they become more than just a wish: they become an unrelenting, burning desire.

Misty Copeland desired to be a ballerina so deeply that she made it happen despite her challenging circumstances. You can do the same if you have the desire and believe you can. Once you fan the flames of desire you gain the power to take action, and this is where the principle of *Faith-Based Action* takes hold.

Many people do not understand that faith can be acquired. You gain more faith when you stay focused on what you could and should have, to the point that you feel waves of joy—as if you have already achieved it. You embrace the necessity of executing all the *Live Ready*® principles to get what you want.

When you choose a *Life Purpose* and focus on positive emotions to seed your subconscious mind, you're putting the rule of *Faith-Based Action* into motion. And this is how you gain the ability to connect to *Infinite Intelligence,* and opportunities appear.

How much time in a day should you dedicate to fanning the flames of your desire and faith?

That depends on you. The more time you spend meditating and focusing on your desires, the more easily you're able to perform the *Faith-Based Action* steps that help you achieve your goal, objective, or *Life Purpose*. You're seeding your mind with the possibility and probability of success.

This is all part of how the *Brain Model* works. As you focus on what you want, you set your RAS to show you the opportunities you have for achieving what you want. This includes the ability to make a practical plan and then put it into action, and it provides the burning desire that inspires you to act with passion and a sense of *Purpose*.

When you are truly acting in faith, you achieve a *Rhythm of Success* the same way Misty Copeland did with ballet. You try hard because dedicated effort is always required. At the same time, you allow yourself to trust and believe that you will achieve what you want. Faith invites you to act with inspiration, and to act immediately.

The sense of trust you feel when you perform *Faith-Based Action* steps is both empowering and liberating, because it frees you from the detrimental effects of fear. Remember, faith is dependent on a *Positive-State-of-Mind*. A *Positive-State-of-Mind* enables you to feel gratitude, both for what you already have and for what you know you can achieve.

Because positive thoughts seed your subconscious with images of success, a faith-filled mind is the opposite of a fear-filled mind. If fear is allowed to run rampant through your mind, it will destroy your faith, and create a *Negative-State-of-Mind* that saps your energy.

All people feel fear, but you don't have to wallow in it. Whenever you begin to feel fear, turn your thoughts and emotions back to what you want and keep them there. Allow yourself to *Pivot to Positive*®, so you can regain your *Thought-Power* to act with faith and motivation. No matter what type of fear you face, that fear cannot hold up against intense faith-thought that is fixed on your goals, objectives, or *Life Purpose* and backed by *Faith-Based Action*.

All you have to do is refuse to think about what you don't want, and instead, focus on everything you do want, with as much passion and burning desire as you can generate. Then you will be so

Nothing happens until an action is put into motion, followed by another one and another one.

motivated that you'll be eager to take action, eager to participate in your own growth, and eager to achieve everything you want.

There's another caution to consider. When you're moving forward toward a goal, objective, or your *Life Purpose,* it's natural to face some challenges and temporary defeat. This happened to Misty Copeland several times—when she didn't have a stable home to support her, when she had to compete with stereotypes, and when she was learning ballet as a latecomer. This didn't stop Misty, and it doesn't have to stop you.

Adversity is not failure unless you accept it as so. Adversity is just a temporary setback requiring adjustments to your *Faith-Based Action* until you regain the *Rhythm of Success*.

Remember, faith is the art of believing by doing, and nothing happens until an action is put into motion, followed by another one and another one. Executing *Faith-Based Actions* is mandatory to *Live Ready*®.

Summary:

The *Faith-Based Action* rule sets the stage for success. As you embrace *Faith-Based Actions*, you properly seed your mind with thoughts for success and develop a pattern of recognizing opportunity. The continual execution of energized actions creates the *Rhythm of Success*.

Faith is the link between *Infinite Intelligence*, the reticular activating system (see the *Brain Model* in Chapter One) and *Faith-Based Action* to get what you want. *Faith-Based Actions* begin when you put a plan into motion, confidently executing all the actions needed to achieve your *Purpose*. When you're acting in faith, you expect success, and you experience one of the most powerful positive mental states achievable.

Faith-Based Action *challenge*

Access QR code at eleadertech.com/FBAC

> *"Before everything else, getting ready is the secret to success"*
>
> — HENRY FORD

CHAPTER FIVE

Readiness Mindset

THE *READINESS MINDSET* PRINCIPLE ENABLES YOU TO create and maintain a *Positive-State-of-Mind.* This positive thought setting ensures your actions are put into motion fully energized, developing *Faith-Based Action.*

When you develop a *Readiness Mindset,* you begin to *Live Ready*®—and the momentum you build makes achieving your goals, objectives, or *Life Purpose* inevitable.

The *Readiness Mindset* principle is like a 7-speed gearbox transmission that regulates your *Brain Model* engine and is powered with *Positive-State-of-Mind* fuel.

The 7 gears of the *Readiness Mindset* principle are:

- **Going the Extra Mile**
- **Personal Initiative**
- **Self-Discipline**
- **Controlled Attention**
- **Controlled Enthusiasm**
- **Accurate Thought**
- **Creative Vision**

Once all seven gears are put into motion, your actions become supercharged with belief, thus becoming *Faith-Based Action.* An action put into motion that is not powered by the *Readiness Mindset* principle will fall short.

THE FIRST GEAR OF THE "READINESS MINDSET" IS
"Going the Extra Mile"

Everybody loves people who do more than they are expected to do, especially when they do it with energy and a smile. When a restaurant server over-delivers, their customers enjoy their dining experience more; even a soft drink seems to taste better when a server goes the extra mile to serve it with a smile. They are always rewarded with the largest tips and the most repeat customers.

Going the Extra Mile requires you to over-deliver on what you agree to do—to give it all you've got. It can be as simple as being the first one at work and the last one to leave, delivering an assignment ahead of schedule, or staying to help others reach their goals. When you're over-delivering, you've developed the habit of exceeding expectations. You will be amazed at how far this first gear will take you in life.

Shifting into the *Extra Mile* gear may be difficult at first—but because it is so satisfying, soon it becomes easier. Once you become the *Switch Master of Your Own Thought*® and *Pivot to Positive*®, you effortlessly shift into the forward motion of the *Going the Extra Mile* gear.

When you give more service than what people expect to receive, you will gain the reputation of being trustworthy, disciplined, and dependable. This sets the stage for your success. The *Going the Extra Mile* gear, when put into motion, never lets you down, and it pays off in proportion to the intensity with which you apply it.

THE SECOND GEAR OF THE "READINESS MINDSET" IS
"Personal Initiative"

TAKEAWAYS

Personal Initiative is that voice in your head, that driving force pushing you to do better and to always improve.

The *Personal Initiative* gear is the twin to the *Going the Extra Mile* gear. Developing the carry-it-through habit—to keep moving forward—no matter what, is key to supercharging your

> **Both your failures and your successes are the result of what you think**

Faith-Based Actions. The most difficult part of any action is to start performing it. If a plan fails, adjust it, and keep moving forward until you achieve your goal, objective, or *Life Purpose*.

The *Personal Initiative* gear generates your power to become a self-starter and to execute *Faith-Based-Actions* to gain the discipline to get thing done.

The *Personal Initiative* gear provides freedom from limitations in your imagination. Those who shift into the *Personal Initiative* gear do not drift, procrastinate, or complain about the lack of opportunities. *Personal Initiative* creates opportunities!

Personal Initiative is that voice in your head, that driving force pushing you to do better and to always improve, from the smallest habit to the largest venture. With *Personal Initiative*, your motives create that inner nudge that urges you to put *Faith-Based-Action* into motion, and nothing happens until you do.

THE THIRD GEAR OF THE "READINESS MINDSET" IS *"Self-Discipline"*

The *Self-Discipline* gear enables you to gain control over everything you think and do. *Self-Discipline* begins when you become the *Switch Master of Your Own Thought*®. Both your failures and your successes are the result of what you think. *Self-Discipline* enables you to control your thoughts and pivot to a *Positive-State-of-Mind*.

The *Self-Discipline* gear, shifted into motion, creates balance of the heart and the head, so neither reasoning nor emotions can dominate the other. *Self-Discipline* is a cornerstone of many worldwide teachings because it allows you to be your best self, become laser-focused, and fan the flames of the desires that inspire you. It helps you master indecision and procrastination, so you can take charge of your thoughts and actions.

Self-Discipline enables you to manage both your joy and fear emotions. Emotions trigger your *State-of-Mind* switches. Some of these emotions consist of the following:

Positive-State-of-Mind – Joy Emotions—love, intimacy, hope, faith, enthusiasm, loyalty, and desire.

Negative-State-of-Mind – Fear Emotions—hate, jealousy, revenge, greed, anger, and superstition, along with the seven basic fears: of not having enough money, criticism, the loss of health, the loss of love, old age, the loss of spare time, and even the fear of death itself.

The *Self-Discipline* gear gives you the ability to control your *State-of-Mind*, direct your thoughts, control your emotions, and take ownership of your results, your direction, and most importantly, your *Purpose*.

THE FOURTH GEAR OF THE "READINESS MINDSET" IS
"Controlled Attention"

The *Controlled Attention* gear coordinates all the powers of the mind and directs their combined power toward the attainment of what you want. *Controlled Attention* cannot be obtained unless the *Self-Discipline* gear has also been shifted into motion as well. Attention that is neither controlled nor directed can be nothing more than a curiosity or a distraction. *Controlled Attention* is the key to the power of thought.

Controlled Attention is organized thought-power. It enables you to focus your thoughts upon the attainment of what you want.

The difference between *Controlled Attention* and attention, which is not controlled, is extreme. It is the difference between feeding your mind with positive thoughts that will get you what you want or allowing your mind to feed upon negative thoughts that will prevent you from getting what you want.

The *Controlled Attention* gear creates the *Readiness Mindset*, replacing negative habits with positive habits, enabling the *Habit of Success* to be realized.

Each day, you should ask yourself many times, "Is this time block helping me or is it distracting me from achieving what I want?"

These questions can help you eliminate the wasteful habits in your life and harness the power of *Controlled Attention*—so focus becomes a natural habit.

THE FIFTH GEAR OF THE "READINESS MINDSET" IS *"Controlled Enthusiasm"*

The *Controlled Enthusiasm* gear is the gateway to all personal achievement. It creates the burning desire to start the success journey. *Controlled Enthusiasm* enables you to use the *Brain Model* process to maintain a *Positive-State-of-Mind*.

True *enthusiasm* comes from within. However, *enthusiasm* is like getting water from a well: first, you must prime the pump, until the water flows and does not stop. You should have *Controlled Enthusiasm* for your *Specialized Talent* and all things you do. *Controlled Enthusiasm* is a *Positive-State-of-Mind* characteristic. It can be generated naturally from one's thoughts, feelings, and emotions, but more importantly, it can become natural and generated at will.

In most cases, the *Controlled Enthusiasm* gear is extremely helpful in the achievement of what you want, but uncontrolled enthusiasm can derail your progress. Uncontrolled enthusiasm creates high energy conversations that may sound good but produce little to no results. Staying grounded in *Controlled Enthusiasm* creates passion and a burning desire toward the achievement of your goals, objectives, or *Life Purpose*.

The *Controlled Enthusiasm* gear regulates your level of influence over yourself and others. It is one of your greatest assets. *Controlled Enthusiasm* thrives while in a *Positive-State-of-Mind,* executing *Faith-Based-Action*.

THE SIXTH GEAR OF THE "READINESS MINDSET" IS
"Accurate Thought"

The *Accurate Thought* gear separates fact from fiction or hearsay. *Accurate Thought* classifies facts into two categories: important or unimportant. While in the *Accurate Thought* gear, you do not accept ideas without analyzing them and then deciding to accept or reject them.

Accurate Thought is based on two major fundamentals.

- **Illogical reasoning**—based on the assumption of unknown facts or hypotheses.
- **Logical reasoning**—based on known facts or what is believed to be facts.

While in the *Accurate Thought* gear, you distinguish facts from mere information or gossip. You become able to reach decisions accurately and quickly. If your thoughts are based on incorrect facts, poor logic, and faulty reasoning, you will be building on a base of sand that will quickly erode under your feet.

One advantage of the *Accurate Thought* gear is that it helps you distinguish negativity from true threats to your progress. It allows you to weigh what you know and believe against the whispers of Dr. Doubt, so you can stay in a *Positive-State-of-Mind* and keep moving forward.

THE SEVENTH GEAR OF THE "READINESS MINDSET" IS
"Creative Vision"

The *Creative Vision* gear makes everything possible. It is the overdrive of the *Readiness Mindset* principle. *Creative Vision* is closely related to the *State-of-Mind* known as faith. It is interesting to note that those who have demonstrated the greatest amount of *Creative Vision* have also displayed an abundance of faith.

Creative Vision is the starting point of all scientific inventions. It describes how old ideas, plans, or concepts can be woven together in a new combination.

For some, *Creative Vision* may be a natural quality of the mind. For others, it can be acquired, and it may be developed by the free and fearless use of the mind's imagination.

One way to increase your *Creative Vision* is by developing the habit of taking time to study, time to think, and time to plan. Be still and listen for that small voice that speaks from within you as you contemplate how you can achieve your goals, objectives, or *Life Purpose*.

Your *Creative Vision* can start as something just for you, then expand into something that can be shared. Your *Creative Vision*, whether small or billion-dollar worthy, is at the heart of everything you do moving forward.

As you shift through these gears, it becomes apparent that they work together to create a powerful momentum toward your goals, objectives, and *Life Purpose*. Just as a car needs every gear for a fully working transmission, you need every *Readiness Mindset* gear, fully engaged and working in tandem with the other gears, to provide you with efficient, effective forward movement.

This is evident in the life of Dr. John Sachtouras, also known as John the Greek and 'the man who never gives up and always keeps moving forward.'

As a multi-million-dollar entrepreneur and renowned worldwide network marketing strategist, John has trained his brain to be in complete control, not only of his thought-habits, but also of his *Readiness Mindset* gears. This empowers him to move forward toward his goals, objectives, and *Life Purpose* at a steady pace, constantly staying in a *Positive-State-of-Mind*. His utilization of the *Readiness Mindset* gears has paid off for him—big time—but it wasn't always easy.

John Sachtouras was born in Greece. Before he immigrated to the United States of America, he worked in the tourism and travel business. Even then, he embraced the belief that appreciating and serving other people would lead to success and happiness. This concept prompted him to *Go the Extra Mile* in all his endeavors, even when times were hard.

In the 1980s, Greece suffered an economic downturn, and the threat of terrorism attacks grew. When the tourism business dropped significantly, John decided it was time for a change.

Beyond Think and Grow Rich **101**

In 1986, at the age of 26, he immigrated to the United States with a burning desire to become a millionaire. He wanted the freedom that money brings. John understood that having money gives you choices and the ability to help others, and he wanted to make a positive difference in the world.

John didn't know how he was going to achieve his *Purpose,* but it was embedded into his heart and mind. He committed to act. He used his *Personal Initiative* to seek income, starting with whatever jobs he could get.

One of his first jobs was as a waiter at an Italian restaurant. It seemed unlikely that anyone would notice his potential in such a setting, but he shifted easily into the *Extra Mile* gear and worked harder than ever. John had the *Self Discipline* to work through both large and small tasks, no matter how difficult—as long as the job was ethical, legal, and allowed him to serve other people.

John's *Positive-State-of-Mind* fueled a burning desire to execute his *Faith-Based Actions,* which propelled him forward toward achieving his goals. He caught the attention of everyone around him.

In 1988, a customer presented John with a flyer for a seminar about network marketing and urged him to attend. Once again, John took the *Personal Initiative* to move forward and investigate this new opportunity. What he found there changed everything.

At the seminar, John sat at the back of the room, trying to grasp what network marketing was all about. He applied the *Readiness Mindset* gear of *Controlled Attention.* His earnest efforts to understand allowed him to become a receiving station for *Infinite Intelligence,* and every idea began to click neatly into place. Concepts such as residual income, the power of diversifying employment level by level, and collecting rewards sparked in his mind, igniting a desire to learn more—and then, to put his newfound knowledge to work.

John was hooked, and he was on fire. From that moment, he attended every seminar and read every book about network marketing he could get, to seed his subconscious mind with *Accurate Thought.* His *Controlled Attention* kept him focused and determined. This clarified his goals, objectives, and *Life Purpose.* He quickly realized that network marketing could be the Big Idea and the driving theme behind becoming a millionaire.

On November 18, 1992, John attended a network marketing event, where he wrote himself a check for one million dollars. He committed himself to doing whatever was necessary to achieve that goal. From studying and learning to becoming a servant leader, he was determined that no matter what, he would achieve his goal, and cash that check.

John understood that achieving his goal would take time. His *Controlled Attention* and *Controlled Enthusiasm* kept him on track, practicing patience as he built his network marketing empire from the ground up.

During his first 20 years, John worked with seventeen network marketing companies. He owned eight businesses personally, with sixty-six retail outlets in seventeen countries. John earned and learned as he went. Not every lesson was easy. On occasion, John hit rock-bottom. He nearly went bankrupt twice. People with a *Negative-State-of-Mind* began appearing in his life. They ridiculed him, criticized his goals, and told him that his efforts were a crazy waste of time.

By now, John had fully engaged all the *Readiness Mindset* gears, including *Accurate Thought*. This allowed him to weigh the words of the naysayers with what he knew about network marketing. John also had the *Creative Vision* to achieve what he wanted, as well as a clear mental image of his own potential. He kept his *Positive-State-of-Mind* and became immune to the criticism.

His steadfast determination and persistence paid off, and his career slowly built momentum. It took John many years to have a yearly income of over $100,000, but soon after that, he was making millions.

Remember the million-dollar check John wrote for himself? He cashed that check exactly 18 years later, and on that day, he also wrote himself a new check. This time, the amount was one billion dollars.

John wanted to experience the feeling of being a multi-millionaire in every way. Soon after he achieved his first million, he had a suitcase full of money brought to him during one of his trade shows. He opened it up and showed the crowd what a million dollars looked like. He felt the crisp edges of the bills and lifted the money so everyone could see.

It was an effective way to motivate the crowd. John challenged the audience, telling them that if he could achieve a million-dollar goal, they could do it, too.

At times like this, John has been heard to quote Napoleon Hill: "Whatever your mind can conceive and believe, it can achieve."

From that moment, his *Creative Vision* exploded. Now that he had experienced what it was like to be a millionaire, he wanted to know what it would look like and feel like to be a billionaire.

He did so at a trade show in Las Vegas. Instead of bringing a briefcase, John's assistants wheeled a safe onto the stage. Piles of money were carted out to show the audience, as well as himself, that the idea of earning millions or even a billion dollars was in fact very possible. It all started by thinking you could. With a strong sense of *Purpose, Faith-Based Action,* and all the *Readiness Mindset* gears engaged, John knew he could achieve anything that he believed.

Reaching that first million-dollar goal was just the beginning. John's determination to serve people combined with his love of network marketing inspired a new *Creative Vision.*

John realized that the goal of earning a billion dollars was not the most important goal. He decided his new goal should be about helping people gain knowledge as an asset, while helping them develop the *Habits of Success*. His new *Creative Vision* was to provide the knowledge, experience, and wisdom to help people improve their lives—and he wanted to help more than a billion people.

His new *Creative Vision* went beyond a Big Idea. It became John's new *Life Purpose.*

John began to crystalize the idea of sharing knowledge as an asset. He wanted to create a new type of network marketing company that could provide professional and personal development to help people jumpstart their lives. The topics would range from beloved hobbies to business and career foundations. People in the business could learn, teach, and take action to improve their own lives and build opportunities for everyone around them.

Once he settled on this as his Big Idea for helping him achieve his new *Life Purpose,* John needed to find a name for it. At first, he thought of Sachtouras Enterprises or Sachtouras Incorporated, but neither name seemed right. He wanted something that portrayed the deep purpose behind the name—to help people learn and achieve their full potential.

John began to write about the company. He documented what the benefits of the company would be, who the company would be for, and why he was forming it. He detailed the benefits participants would receive and even wrote questions and answers about the company that he could share with others.

As he looked over what he wrote, he realized that some key words appeared repeatedly. Those words, and the ideas behind them, developed the acronym that became the company name.

- **A**ttitude – developing a *Positive-State-of-Mind* life setting. If you don't have positive thoughts, you will not succeed.
- **S**ystem – to create long lasting success, you must have a winning system in place.
- **C**ommitment – you can have all the above, but there will be things that don't go right, and you will have to be committed to adjust and continue your success journey. You must be committed to your future.
- **I**ntegrity – if things do not work perfectly, you will be confronted with choices, and you must do the right thing every time, no matter what it costs you. Integrity can never be compromised.
- **R**ecognition – this company would be the business of people, with a focus on building and developing people. Success is built with Capital and People Talent—you must have both to create success—but People ARE the most important ingredient, and it's important to recognize *Extra Mile* efforts.
- **A**ccountability – be accountable for your actions.

Using the first letter of those keywords, John formed the word ASCIRA, which became the name for his new company. Besides the

Purpose of reaching beyond a billion people in the ASCIRA community, he also set a company goal: to reach 100 countries, with 1,000 network marketers achieving Diamond status, within just 10 years.

As of 2022, John is the CEO of this breakthrough global network marketing company. ASCIRA is designed and structured to empower people by sharing priceless knowledge and education with them.

Through ASCIRA and other platforms, John shares the concepts he lives by: faith, belief, action, and determination, with a strong focus on persistence and serving each other. His official website specifically emphasizes the importance of a never-give-up attitude—which is exactly what the *Readiness Mindset* gears provide.

John calls ASCIRA the company "For the People." Its purpose is to share the gift and power of knowledge, allowing all participants to improve themselves and connect with others in a mutually beneficial way. Through ASCIRA, people seeking knowledge have a new opportunity to gain the knowledge they seek—which, sometimes, is unattainable to them from other sources or is too expensive to access.

Because they're learning what they want to learn, people are excited about it, and they share the company's services with other people. Every time they share the company's services with a new customer, they get paid, so they are earning money while at the same time, learning and improving their quality of life.

Meanwhile, ASCIRA pays the teachers, who are professional content providers, top authors, and other experts from diverse industries. Rather than searching for more funding, they can spend their time doing what they do well: sharing knowledge.

John Sachtouras believes that gaining knowledge is the key to achieving what you want in life. He believes that everybody has a superpower, but most people don't know how to tap into it. ASCIRA helps ordinary people overcome their limitations, elevate their mindsets, and improve their lives, so they can reach their potential.

TAKEAWAYS

Controlled Success: In the beginning stages of your success journey, it's important to ask for assistance to help replace bad habits with good ones.

John Sachtouras has been a network marketing expert for 30 plus years, with seventeen companies and over one million network followers—and ASCIRA is projected to be his next big success.

Through the years, John has achieved his goals, objectives, and *Life Purpose* by persistently focusing on them. He kept that focus strong by using all the *Readiness Mindset* gears to energize his *Faith-Based Actions*.

The *Brain,* powered by a *Positive-State-of-Mind* and seeded with the right thoughts, is essential for you to achieve your goals, objectives, or *Life Purpose*. Utilizing all seven *Readiness Mindset* gears makes it possible for you to maximize the *Brain Model* engine to supercharge your *Faith-Based Actions* before you put them into motion. Like John, you too can use the *Readiness Mindset* principle to achieve whatever you think and believe—so how do you start?

In the beginning stages of your success journey, it's important to ask for assistance to help replace bad habits with good ones. This is known as the *Controlled Success* stage. While the word 'control' is not inviting to most, *Controlled Success* is necessary for everyone who wishes to change something about themselves that holds them back from achieving their *Purpose*.

Controlled Success happens when you invite a mentor or coach to help you. They provide the accountability and guidance you need, while you develop the *Self-Discipline* to repeatedly execute your *Faith-Based Actions*. As you perform those actions over and over again, it begins to feel like a rhythm—and you've entered the next stage, which is the *Rhythm of Success*

When you've had the *Self-Discipline* to execute your *Faith-Based Actions* in the *Rhythm of Success* for hundreds of days, you will slowly notice powerful shifts in your actions. Your results improve, and you will ascend to the final stage, the *Habit of Success*.

To achieve the *Habit of Success,* you must be willing to invite *Controlled Success* into your life. Besides requiring a coach or mentor, you must move the *Readiness Mindset* gears into action. It is imperative that you create a personal *Readiness Mindset* exercise that you do every morning.

For example, my *Readiness Mindset* exercise is folded into my morning routine. I start by listening to five minutes of something inspirational, such as *Think and Grow Rich,* on my shower speaker. This helps me wake up both my mind and body with something invigorating and exciting, and it engages the *Readiness Mindset* gears of *Controlled Attention, Controlled Enthusiasm,* and *Accurate Thought.*

The next step requires that I look in the mirror and repeat my *Purpose* statement, with enthusiasm. Then I review my business initiatives. These steps kick the *Readiness Mindset* gear of *Personal Initiative* into motion.

Next, I open my calendar to see who I'm meeting with that day. My clients have honored me by asking me to mentor or coach them, and I'd better honor them by being ready to deliver. Scanning my calendar and anticipating a positive outcome with each client engages the *Readiness Mindset* gears of *Going the Extra Mile* and *Creative Visualization.*

Once I've scanned my calendar and visualized those appointments in a *Positive-State-of-Mind,* I move to my goal statement. These are the measurements for the standards I've set for myself, in the areas of family/friends, faith, community, health, and financial wealth. I ask myself, "What do I want, and how am I going to measure myself against those standards—TODAY?"

With my goal statements in mind, I review my daily, weekly, and monthly plan for *Faith-Based Actions.* I read them out loud to seed my subconscious with the *Readiness Mindset* gear of *Self-Discipline,* so I can get things done.

This chapter is key. Nothing happens until you gain the *Self-Discipline* and engage the other *Readiness Mindset* gears to get things done.

The first five *Live Ready*® principles are essential to your success. Mastering the remaining *Live Ready*® principles guarantee your success. Let's review these five core principles.

TAKEAWAYS

The first five *Live Ready*® principles are essential to your success. Mastering the remaining *Live Ready*® principles guarantee your success.

Principle One – *Positive-State-of-Mind:*
We discussed the power of a positive thought setting and using the *Brain Model* to become the *Switch Master of Your Own Thought*® and *Pivot-to-Positive*®.

Principle Two – *Purpose:*
We challenged you to ask yourself a simple question—what is it that you want? If you haven't determined a *Life Purpose,* start with a goal or an objective.

Principle Three – *Specialized Talent Team:*
You must determine the talent you need to accomplish what you want. List the skills you have and take note of the ones you don't have. Then add those missing skills and talents by building a *Specialized Talent Team.*

Principle Four – *Faith-Based Actions:*
Develop *Faith-Based Actions* to build your momentum. Commit to do these actions repetitively to create a *Readiness Mindset* and ultimately the *Habit of Success.*

Principle Five – *Readiness Mindset:*
Conquering this principle enables you to manage the *Brain Model* engine and constantly fuel it with a *Positive-State-of-Mind.*

Your personal *Readiness Mindset* exercise seeds your subconscious mind with *Self-Discipline* and the other *Readiness Mindset* gears, so you can get what you could and should have in life. To move forward and build momentum, you should do your *Readiness Mindset* exercise every day, for the rest of your life.

If you do, you will *Live Ready*®.

Now, rev up your *Brain Model* engine by creating your personal *Readiness Mindset* exercise that utilizes all seven *Readiness Mindset* gears. Power it with *Positive-State-of-Mind* fuel and make all your *Faith-Based Actions* supercharged.

Summary:

The *Readiness Mindset* principle is like a gearbox that regulates the *Brain Model* engine.

In the beginning stages of your success journey, it's important to ask for assistance to help replace bad habits with good ones. This is known as the *Controlled Success* stage. As you perform those actions with repetition you'll enter the next stage, the *Rhythm of Success*. After hundreds of days in the *Rhythm of Success*, you will ascend to the final stage, the *Habit of Success*.

These *Readiness Mindset* gears can be activated by developing a daily readiness exercise to ensure all your *Faith-Based Actions* are supercharged and executed with meaning.

Readiness Mindset *challenge*

Access QR code or at eleadertech.com/RMC

> "I've learned that people will forget what you said, people will forget what you did, but people will never forget how you made them feel."
>
> — MAYA ANGELOU

CHAPTER SIX

Pleasing Personality

YOUR PERSONALITY IS YOUR GREATEST ASSET OR your greatest liability. It shapes the nature of your thoughts and actions. It strengthens or weakens your relationships with family, friends, work team members, and everyone you meet. Your personality is like your fingerprints: it defines the uniqueness of you as a person—good or bad.

The way you make people feel is vital to *Living Ready*. The *Pleasing Personality* principle of being considerate and thoughtful in all your relationships can determine if you win or lose the game of life.

This chapter is the equivalent of a complete course on marketing, because obtaining a *Pleasing Personality* enables you to present your ideas successfully. It ignites the power of harmonious attraction and activates your ability to gain cooperation from both capital and talent partners to achieve a worthy cause. A *Pleasing Personality* lays the foundation for leadership.

Your personality is the sum-total of your mental, spiritual, and physical traits that distinguish you from all others. It is the factor that determines whether you are liked or disliked.

It is the medium by which you will negotiate your way through

Beyond Think and Grow Rich

life. And it will determine whether you are able to maintain harmony in your interactions with others.

The financial value of a *Pleasing Personality* may be measured by observing those who have a disagreeable personality. They are seldom found in positions of leadership or wealth. Those with a *Pleasing Personality* build strong relationships while marketing themselves and their ideas. Those with a disagreeable personality most often have weak relationships and no-one wants to listen to them or their ideas.

Those that master the *Brain Model* lesson—covered in chapter one—maintain a positive mind setting and naturally display a *Pleasing Personality*.

Characteristics of a *Pleasing Personality* include a *Positive-State-of-Mind*, decisiveness, flexibility, sincerity, courtesy, tactfulness, patience, controlled emotions, genuine smile, pleasant tone of voice, and kindness.

Let's discuss the characteristics of a *Pleasing Personality* in more detail.

A Positive-State-of-Mind

— To understand the importance of a *Positive-State-of-Mind,* consider the fact that it affects your tone of voice, your facial expression, your body posture, your thoughts, and the words you use. It seeds the emotions of joy and belief into your subconscious. A *Positive-State-of-Mind* equals a *Pleasing Personality,* and a *Negative-State-of-Mind* equals a disagreeable personality. Every person you meet will feel or see one of these two personalities within you. You choose which one you display.

TAKEAWAYS

The *Pleasing Personality* principle of being considerate and thoughtful in all your relationships can determine if you win or lose the game of life.

The value of a *Pleasing Personality* may be measured by observing those who have a disagreeable personality. They are easy to identify at any function. They are the people who are standing all alone.

A *Pleasing Personality* creates the positive personal characteristics which attract people to you. It enables you to obtain their favorable

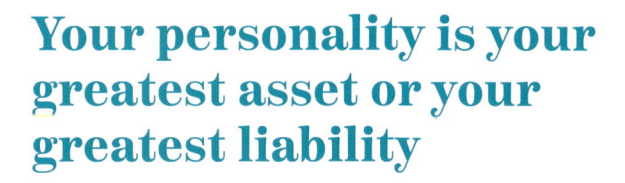

Your personality is your greatest asset or your greatest liability

cooperation for the achievement of your goals, objectives, or *Life Purpose*. A *Pleasing Personality* is a natural characteristic of those who have achieved and maintain a *Positive-State-of-Mind* thought setting.

Decisiveness — *Decisiveness* is a habit that springs from your sincerity, conviction, and dedication to your *Life Purpose*. With your *Purpose* seeded into your subconscious mind, and backed by *Faith-Based Action*, it becomes clear how to get what you want—and the ability to quickly make sound decisions becomes natural.

Acquiring the habit of sound, quick decision-making requires *Self-Discipline, Controlled Attention, Accurate Thinking,* and a *Positive-State-of-Mind*. These *Live Ready*® principles help build the *Rhythm of Success* and eventually the *Habit of Success*.

Flexibility — *Flexibility* is the habit of seeking to understand someone else's belief or point of view before you offer your own. You do not have to accept or agree with every new idea to achieve the flexibility characteristic, but it does require a positive thought setting in all discussions.

Flexibility allows you to maintain *Accurate Thought,* while embracing your ability to understand and invite conversation from other perspectives. When your *Specialized Talent Team* exercises the flexibility habit during team discussion, they often enter the *Genius Zone* to discover Big Ideas. This process enables them to influence talent partners, capital partners, and community leaders to achieve their goals, objectives, or *Life Purpose*.

The flexibility habit also has value in the achievement of success in business, family/friends, faith, community, health, and financial wealth.

Sincerity – *Sincerity* is the habit of being genuine and authentic in every interaction. No one likes a fake. Sincerity requires a high level of personal integrity. When you are sincere, your *Faith-Based Actions* match perfectly with your core beliefs.

Sincerity creates trust, which impacts your relationships within all walks of life. The payoff is enormous.

It influences the way capital partners, talent partners, and customers interact with you. It embraces your ability to create value and *Positive-State-of-Mind* feelings in every conversation you have—and the feelings you create in others are everlasting.

Sincerity develops self-confidence. When you are sincere, your faith in yourself is obvious. You radiate confidence in all your actions, backed by your belief in your goals, objectives, or *Life Purpose*.

Courtesy – *Courtesy* is the most profitable trait of a *Pleasing Personality*, and it is available to you free of charge. It is the habit of respecting other people under every circumstance, helping people less fortunate than you, serving without the thought of a reward, and controlling your own negative emotions by pivoting to a positive thought setting.

From a financial standpoint, courtesy is completely free, so it can be given freely to all. To be courteous, you must maintain a *Positive-State-of-Mind*, as well as sincerity, consideration for the well-being of others, and a willingness to share your blessings. All these requirements are interrelated, so developing in one area helps you develop in all the areas.

One advantage of courtesy is that it can disarm adversaries and competitors. It can also enhance harmony within a *Specialized Talent Team*. *Courtesy* is an irresistible force, and it is essential for inspiring the cooperation of others.

TAKEAWAYS

When your **Specialized Talent Team** exercises the flexibility habit during team discussion, they often enter the *Genius Zone* to discover Big Ideas.

Tactfulness – *Tactfulness* is closely related to courtesy, but it has more to do with the way you speak than the way you

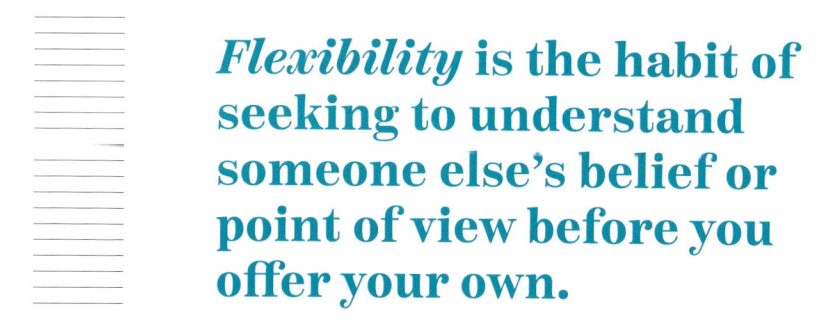

> ***Flexibility* is the habit of seeking to understand someone else's belief or point of view before you offer your own.**

act. Tactfulness consists of doing and saying the right things, at the right time, in the right way, to build cooperation and harmony.

Tactfulness is grounded in sincerity, and it sometimes requires an honest discussion of areas where improvements are needed. However, because tactfulness embraces the consideration of others, any constructive criticism must be delivered in a way that builds harmony and trust. Courtesy and tactfulness are so closely related that they are often used together to help inspire the support of others.

Patience – *Patience* is the ability to maintain a *Positive-State-of-Mind,* often while enduring challenges or waiting for the results of your hard work. Being patient provides several rewards, including the ability to maintain a calm, confident disposition in any circumstance. It suggests the idea that success is inevitable.

It's imperative to keep your body healthy and your mind relaxed. As you develop patience, you gain wisdom for achieving your goals, objectives, and *Life Purpose.*

Controlled Emotions – Emotions control our thoughts, actions, and behavior. Most people are controlled by their emotions, rather than controlling them. In the final analysis, we all do what we want to do, based on the negative or positive emotions seeded into our subconscious—as per the *Brain Model* covered in chapter one.

When you develop a *Pleasing Personality,* you utilize *Self-Discipline* to train your mind and body. You allow yourself to demonstrate the emotions that help convey your message, so you can empower others and build harmony in all your interactions.

Genuine Smile — Smiling is an essential part of a *Pleasing Personality* for several reasons. Smiling helps relax the body, lower the heart rate, reduce blood pressure, and decrease stress levels. When you're walking into a tense situation, smiling helps you and the people around you to pivot to a positive thought setting, so you can make decisions that lead to success.

Science has proven that smiling is contagious. When you smile at someone, their mirror neurons kick in, and they feel compelled to smile back. The result is that everyone who is sharing a smile enjoys a powerful boost of the *Brain Model's* DOSE chemicals: dopamine, oxytocin, serotonin, and endorphins. Besides relieving stress and tension, the DOSE chemicals can help combat anxiety and depression, so that all team members can work happily and harmoniously in the *Genius Zone*.

Pleasant Tone of Voice — A *pleasant tone of voice* conveys meaning that goes beyond the words you say. The tone you speak in reveals your emotions, good or bad. The person with a *Pleasing Personality* understands how to effectively communicate those emotions, by modifying voice tone to support and empower the people they are communicating with.

Your tone of voice can express a wide range of emotions. While some tones portray fear, anger, or doubt, other tones communicate courage, sincerity, and conviction. Patient practice results in the ability to put your pleasant tone of voice to work for you, so you can demonstrate harmony in all your interactions.

TAKEAWAYS

Conversations held while in a **Pleasing Personality** normally result in decisions that lead to success. Conversations held while in a disagreeable personality—most often—will result in decisions that lead to failure.

Kindness — Everyone enjoys being around those who naturally like people because they can feel their kindness. Like

Everyone enjoys being around those who naturally like people because they can feel their kindness.

a magnet, kind people attract others to them, so kind people are seldom seen alone.

The greatest personal compliment you can offer is to focus your attention on someone else. When you like people, you are interested in them. You listen to them, take time for them, and do what you can to serve them—resulting in kindness and a powerful *Pleasing Personality*.

High-end business success requires associates to exhibit a *Pleasing Personality,* for it impacts productivity, customer satisfaction, team turnover and bottom-line profit. Conversations held while in a *Pleasing Personality* normally result in decisions that lead to success. Conversations held while in a disagreeable personality—most often—will result in decisions that lead to failure. A *Pleasing Personality* culture attracts the most talented people to your organization. Top tier talent wants to work with a *Purpose* driven leader who has a *Pleasing Personality*.

Let me share a story of how one company built their success using their collective *Pleasing Personality* to out-serve and out-care their competition.

Their story began at the end of World War II, when S. Truett Cathy returned from the war to his hometown, Atlanta, Georgia USA. He didn't have a fully developed purpose let alone a Big Idea of how to achieve success, but he did have an impeccable character. Truett Cathy was a hard worker who was generous, confident, and inspiring. He started with a simple goal: he wanted to provide financially for his family, while making life better for everyone he met.

Rather than hunting for employment, he chose to start his own business. He and his brother, Ben, opened a tiny diner—the Dwarf House Grill on the outskirts of Atlanta.

Truett Cathy's commitment to his ability to out-serve and out-care others in the restaurant business required a strong core belief, which can only be attained by living in a *Positive-State-of-Mind*. In his gentle, humble way, Truett Cathy was packed with unyielding self-confidence. Even with no Big Idea in mind, his confidence and *Pleasing Personality* gave him the courage to start his journey to success.

At that time, his *Business Purpose* was to sell good food, provide good service, and out-care all his competitors to fulfill his goal of providing for his family.

Like many other *Pure Non-Drifters*, Truett Cathy was sincerely fond of people. He insisted on a lifestyle that would allow him to serve others. This was one of the characteristics of a *Pleasing Personality* that set him apart from most ordinary restaurant owners.

Offering good food as well as service with a smile and a pleasant personality helped fulfill part of his goal. However, a problem was quickly unveiled: the diner was too small. There were only a few tables. It didn't take long before he realized that no matter how full the diner was, it couldn't provide him with a return that could support his family, let alone his brother's family, too.

Once he realized this, he acted promptly, opening a second restaurant that he hoped could meet the financial demands of both families and the families of their team members. He invested in equipment and furnishings, but before long, a fire burned it to the ground.

While others may have lost their way and given up, Truett Cathy pivoted to a positive thought setting. He remained true to his ideals and the *Think and Grow Rich Principles* of Dr. Napoleon Hill, whom he thought of as a mentor. As he pivoted, he found himself able to control his dominating thoughts. He focused positively on his core *Purpose* and chose to work even harder at the first restaurant, confident that another opportunity would reveal itself.

Truett Cathy waited patiently, with hope and ambition, and remained centered on serving people. He seeded his thoughts to hunt for a new opportunity. Soon, opportunity number three appeared, and he made a prompt decision to move forward without delay.

By this time, Truett Cathy knew he needed a Big Idea, and he was on the hunt for it. He understood this idea must have the power to make his restaurants stand out. He created a third restaurant with a homestyle-themed experience, in which customers could prepare their own plates, family style. His Big Idea immediately caught the attention of others. People were curious about the smorgasbord-type restaurant, and they came to experience it.

Business started off with a bang, but it was not sustained. Not everyone was as flexible in their thinking as Truett Cathy thought they would be. At this time in history, customers wanted and expected table service. Although some great articles were written about him and his idea, the customers did not accept his family style self-service theme. Business tapered off, and a return on his investment was not realized. It became obvious his Big Idea was not going to work. He found somebody to take over the location, sold the equipment, and went back to his first restaurant in Atlanta.

Once again, he immersed himself in hard work and stayed centered in a *Positive-State-of-Mind*. In his humble, sincere way, he was determined to figure out a better Big Idea that would allow him to serve others while financially providing for the people closest to him.

His perseverance paid off. One day, a friend came to him with an abundance of grade-A chicken fillets that he couldn't use. This friend was in the business of providing in-flight dining for airplanes, and he bought the chicken fillets to serve there. However, the chicken fillets did not fit the trays in which they were served. He didn't know what to do with them—until he remembered that Truett Cathy had a diner.

Truett Cathy bought them and settled on a way to cook them: his mother's southern fried chicken recipe. He quickly got the recipe, put the ingredients together, and fried up some chicken fillets. He had some of his customers taste-test them, and they simply said—WOW.

His next challenge was figuring out how to present an appealing entrée out of the chicken fillets. Truett Cathy decided to serve them on a bun, much like the hamburgers he served. This idea was partially inspired by some of his customers, who he had seen making sandwiches out of the chicken and rolls he served. His generous nature made it easy for him to give customers what they wanted—chicken sandwiches—and to serve them in a courteous, enthusiastic way that made every customer feel special.

He also created a name for his special chicken fillet sandwiches by spelling fillet as Fil-A, representing the fact that the chicken fillets were grade-A, and that his customers were worth grade-A products.

As he made these changes, his alert interest in his customers paid off. He realized that serving others was a labor of love for him. It was tied into his *Life Purpose*, but it also gave life to his *Business Purpose*: Truett Cathy was going to out-serve and out-care his competition.

From that point, his *Pleasing Personality* laid the foundation for his new *Business Purpose*. It also became the theme for his Big Idea—grade-A chicken sandwiches, served in a way that celebrated each customer as being unique, important, and cared for.

Chick-Fil-A was born. Truett Cathy's *Pleasing Personality* and focus on his *Life Purpose* created a newly themed Big Idea, which attracted an unending stream of customers. His hard work, dedication, and constant consideration for others finally paid off.

People loved Chick-Fil-A. Before long, he opened a second location, and a third. Over time, Chick-Fil-A became one of the most profitable fast-food restaurants in America. Currently, Chick-Fil-A brings in over $8 million annually per location, compared to McDonald's, which brings in approximately $3 million annually per location.

Truett Cathy's dedication to out-serve and out-care his competition was woven into every guest interaction. It started with his own *Pleasing Personality*, but it extended to the Chick-Fil-A team members, who also served with *Pleasing Personalities*. When people are served by someone like Truett Cathy, or his team members, they just leave feeling good. And when you make someone feel good, they never forget you.

Truett Cathy's focus on *Pleasing Personalities* helped Chick-Fil-A gain a reputation of simply out-serving and out-caring their competition. The feeling of a team *Pleasing Personality* made an enormous impact on Chick-Fil-A guests and the communities Chick-Fil-A stores are located in.

The focus on *Pleasing Personalities* is evident in Chick-Fil-A's marketing strategy. Some Chick-Fil-A commercials promote a feel-good, laugh-out-loud companionship with the guests they serve—as they share their healthy sense of humor based around cows prompting customers to 'Eat Mor Chikin.'

Other Chick-Fil-A commercials focus on the people themselves—the team members, the guests, and how they brighten lives together.

Going back into the 1980s, commercials showed families enjoying time together, such as a mother and daughter shopping for a wedding dress and then eating together at Chick-Fil-A. Recent commercials are based on real-life experiences, including a time when Chick-Fil-A team members hosted a birthday party for a Chick-Fil-A guest turning 100 years old. In another example, a Chick-Fil-A team member changed a tire for an exhausted mother, while she and her five children dined. Other commercials feature Chick-Fil-A team members supporting a boy who wanted to feed the homeless, extending Family Night hours to accommodate a single mother, and bringing Chick-Fil-A food to the hospital, where a regular customer had just had a baby.

Most of the Chick-Fil-A commercials are built around stellar customer service, which is achieved by using the *Pleasing Personality* traits. To join the Chick-Fil-A team, candidates must have a *Positive-State-of-Mind* and a *Pleasing Personality*. They must also be willing to embrace the Chick-Fil-A theme of out-serving and out-caring their competition.

Using the principles found in *Think and Grow Rich*, Truett Cathy achieved a successful business model that provided financially for all Chick-Fil-A team members and their families, while promoting a feel-good atmosphere for everyone. He often quoted Napoleon Hill, saying "Anything you can conceive and believe, you can achieve." At an annual convention, he once told Chick-Fil-A managers that the only two books they ever need to read are the Holy Bible and *Think and Grow Rich*, and he stated over and over again that Chick-Fil-A would NEVER be open on Sundays.

True to his convictions, Chick-Fil-A is always closed on Sundays. Despite the loss of a full sales day every week, Chick-Fil-A has become one of the most successful fast-food restaurants in America.

This level of distinction was possible because Truett Cathy themed his Big Idea around out-serving and out-caring their competition, based on the principle of a *Pleasing Personality*. Only a few other establishments have been able to create such unique themed environments.

I list Farrells' Restaurant and Ice Cream Parlour among them. I remember the feeling I had as I recited the Farrell's themed *Purpose* statement—*Farrell's features fabulous food and fantastic fountain fantasies for frolicking fun filled festive families.* It seeded my mind both with the *Purpose* and a *Pleasing Personality*, so I could deliver on that *Purpose* effectively. It helped me to grow tremendously as an individual, but it also unified the Farrells' team, and it created an atmosphere where customers truly enjoyed themselves.

Consider Disneyland, which is themed around providing family fun. Tesla meets people at their homes to work on car issues, and Southwest surprises customers with humor and fun-filled announcements to make flyers smile or laugh.

Like Chick-Fil-A, most companies that obtain a high level of success require an equally high level of guest service from their team members—and that always comes back to the principle of a *Pleasing Personality*. Leaders who develop and encourage *Pleasing Personality* traits create a powerful, influential, and lucrative company culture.

There's one more thing to say about companies that build a culture around the principle of a *Pleasing Personality*. These are the companies that thrive when other companies struggle to survive.

Consider the economic chaos that ensued when the Covid-19 pandemic hit. People—including both guests and company team members—stayed home. Many fast-food establishments shut down because they couldn't find people to work.

That wasn't the case with Chick-Fil-A.

TAKEAWAYS

If you are in a **Positive-State-of-Mind**, it is impossible for you to have a disagreeable personality. If you're in a **Negative-State-of-Mind**, it is impossible for you to achieve a **Pleasing Personality**.

If you are in a *Positive-State-of-Mind*, it is impossible for you to have a disagreeable personality.

While most restaurants struggled to survive, there was always a line at Chick-Fil-A drive up windows. The Chick-Fil-A team members showed up smiling and ready to out-serve and out-care with all their hearts. Positive people want to be around other positive people who have *Pleasing Personalities,* and that shows up both with team members and guests alike. The *Pleasing Personality* culture provides stability and economic growth.

This is what most businesses strive for. If you theme the *Pleasing Personality* rule into your business culture—like Truett Cathy and Robert E. Farrell did—your business can also achieve extraordinary success.

So, where do you start?

In the previous chapters, we've discussed five key principles that help build the *Rhythm of Success* and the *Habit of Success*. Together, those principles move you into a *Success Mindset*, so a *Pleasing Personality* becomes automatic.

If you are in a *Positive-State-of-Mind*, it is impossible for you to have a disagreeable personality. If you're in a *Negative-State-of-Mind*, it is impossible for you to achieve a *Pleasing Personality*.

The fundamentals of a *Pleasing Personality* form a stand-alone philosophy that allows you to reshape your interactions with others. The easiest way to begin developing these fundamentals is by focusing on developing a *Positive-State-of-Mind*. When you do this, many of the other elements that make up a *Pleasing Personality* become natural to you.

It's clear that your *Personality* can be your greatest asset—or your greatest liability. It encompasses everything under your control: body, mind, and soul. Incorporating all aspects of a *Pleasing Personality* helps you establish proper boundaries, form deep and meaningful relationships, and gives you the ability to work in harmony with others.

When you develop a company culture around a *Positive-State-of-Mind,* and it is accompanied by a *Pleasing Personality*—you begin to *Live Ready*®.

Summary:

Your personality is your greatest asset, and it can also be your greatest liability. It shapes your thoughts, actions, and relationships with others. Your personality is the sum-total of your mental, spiritual, and physical traits that distinguish you from all others. It is the factor that determines whether you are liked or disliked. When you develop a *Pleasing Personality,* you also develop the power to make other people feel good—and people always remember how you make them feel.

High end businesses realize the financial value of *Pleasing Personality* traits to help them create unique, themed customer experiences. Teams that demonstrate *Pleasing Personality* traits impact productivity, team turnover, customer satisfaction, and bottom-line profit. Creating a *Pleasing Personality* culture attracts the most talented team members to your organization, so you can make a powerful positive impact on everyone you meet.

Readiness Mindset *challenge*

Access QR code
or at eleadertech.com/PPC

> *"Show me someone who has done something worthwhile, and I'll show you someone who has overcome adversity."*
>
> — LOU HOLTZ

CHAPTER SEVEN

Adversity Adjustment

AS YOU EXECUTE YOUR PLANS TO ACHIEVE YOUR goals, objectives, or *Life Purpose,* there will be times you experience adversity. As in every success journey, life has its ups and downs. No matter how strong your *Success Mindset* is, sometimes things just don't go the way you planned. Steve Jobs was fired from Apple, the very company he created, but he returned to save Apple and redefine the way we use technology. Elon Musk's first three SpaceX rocket launches failed. Fortunately, the fourth launch was a success because the company was nearly out of money. Adversity can block you from getting what you want, or it can simply be an adjustment.

Adversity Adjustment is the pivot point within the *Live Ready® principles of success.* This chapter will show you how to use adversity to pause, adjust your plan, and move forward. You will learn that adversity is not failure unless you accept it as so. *Adversity Adjustments* can create the highest level of success.

The *Adversity Adjustment* principle shows you how to remove limitations that are seeded into your subconscious as the result of believing adversity is failure. It proves adversity is not final unless you accept it as final. This rule proves that every form of adversity brings with it the seed of a greater benefit—but you must learn to look for it.

Simply put, you and everyone else will experience a certain amount of adversity. We can all find courage and inspiration in knowing that every adversity carries with it the seed of a greater benefit. Adversity offers an opportunity to gain knowledge from the adjustments made and executed to obtain your goals, objectives, or *Life Purpose*.

In previous chapters you learned people are divided into two groups—even when it comes to facing adversity:

"Pure Non-Drifters" learn from *Adversity Adjustments*. They expect adversity—they welcome it—knowing the adjustments created by adversity are part of the success process. They have absolute belief in the discovery of a greater benefit.

"Drifters" lack self-discipline and persistence. They are often good starters but poor finishers. Most *Drifters* give up at the first sign of adversity. They accept it as failure, which pivots them into a *Negative-State-of-Mind*, where negative attracts more negative. *Drifters* listen to the whispers of Dr. Doubt and are quick to believe success was never meant for them anyway.

During the 2020 pandemic, it was hard for many people, worldwide, to maintain a *Positive-State-of-Mind* and overcome the adversity facing every person on earth. Yet, even during the pandemic adversity, the seeds of a positive benefit were discovered:

TAKEAWAYS

The **Adversity Adjustment** principle shows you how to remove limitations that are seeded into your subconscious as the result of believing adversity is failure. It proves adversity is not final unless you accept it as final.

- **Instant global conversations became the norm**. We learned that we did not have to be physically sitting in front of someone to effectively communicate. Various online video communication software solutions taught us how to use technology to communicate; to share ideas and have meaningful conversations instantly.

We can all find courage and inspiration in knowing that every adversity carries with it the seed of a greater benefit.

- Many countries developed **effective processes to combat the pandemic** and shared those processes with the world.
- Some factories **retooled their facilities** to build needed medical equipment for hospitals around the globe, keeping people employed.
- Many countries were able to **streamline the coronavirus-testing process** to help effectively and efficiently control the pandemic.
- The world was introduced to **everyday protective procedures** that will undoubtedly be used to combat future viruses or even the flu and common cold.
- Many learned to care for others, **even when these practices were often inconvenient**, and they received criticism from non-believers.

The compensating benefits of *Adversity Adjustments* often cannot be seen as benefits until you look back at these experiences over time. There is no evidence to disprove the fact that every adversity carries with it the seed of a greater benefit.

The central theme of this *Live Ready*® principle may be stated in a simple sentence: While everyone will undergo a certain amount of adversity, everyone can find comfort in the knowledge that *Adversity Adjustment* is necessary for obtaining what you could and should have in life.

For most, *Adversity Adjustment* is the hardest *Live Ready*® principle to master. They see adversity as proof that success was not meant for them. Most have never been introduced to the *Adversity Adjustment* process. *Adversity Adjustment* is the pivot point within the *Live Ready® principles of success.*

Everyone will confront adversity. The key is, will you stop, or adjust and move forward? While the adjustment experience can be humbling, you gain wisdom and understanding in the process.

Recognition of this fact will mark one of the most important milestones in your life since it will lead you to the astounding discovery that adversity does not need to be accepted as failure. *Adversity Adjustments* prove to be blessings in disguise.

Every highly successful person has experienced adversity comparable to their level of success. *Adversity Adjustments* are merely exercises to permit you to discover the source and the nature of your personal *Thought-Power*.

Remember: *Adversity is never the same as failure unless you have accepted it as such.*

Adversity always carries the seed of a greater benefit—but there is no guarantee you will achieve that benefit. You must learn to see the opportunities that adversity presents, and then nurture them, because opportunities are the seeds of greater benefit. Cultivate them with a goal, objective, or *Life Purpose*. As you work with the opportunities that adversity presents to you, they will sprout, spring up, and bear fruit. This is a law of nature.

If you are overwhelmed by circumstances that feel like failures, remember—you may be face-to-face with your greatest opportunity yet. Look for a new vision, a new Big Idea, or a new way to win—and win big.

TAKEAWAYS

When you believe in your own potential, you welcome the *Adversity Adjustment* principle with determination and confidence, and you Live Ready®.

No matter how frustrated adversity may cause you to feel, welcome the *Adversity Adjustment* rule process. Even at your lowest point, executing *Adversity Adjustment* with *Faith-Based Actions* replaces doubt with a positive mindset. This is where you begin the process of correction to welcome your adversity and find its benefit.

The *Adversity Adjustment* principle works in every area of life.

Use your creative imagination to focus on all the positive outcomes, and do not imagine any negative outcomes—remember like attracts like—so be careful what you think. Most often, focusing on those tiny seeds of positive potential will be your starting point. Once you begin, your reticular activating system will kick in. You'll become a receiving station for *Infinite Intelligence,* and more ideas will flow to you. Before long, your plan will become clear.

The final step to executing *Adversity Adjustment* is to follow through with the *Faith-Based Actions* necessary to make the adjustment. As you execute the *Adversity Adjustment* rule this way, you'll discover a greater benefit in every difficult situation. This is an unchangeable principle, a law of nature that you can put to work to help you get what you want in life—even when at times it seems impossible.

Despite the soundness of this rule, few people welcome adversity as a necessary adjustment opportunity. They allow fear and doubt to stop them and accept adversity as final.

Consider what would happen if Olympic athletes decided that difficult training schedules were too challenging for them. They wouldn't even try. That doesn't happen because Olympic athletes embrace the challenge. They understand that it provides them the opportunity to compete and win on an epic scale.

The *Adversity Adjustment* principle works in every area of life. When you believe in your own potential, you welcome the *Adversity Adjustment* principle with determination and confidence, and you *Live Ready*®.

At times *Adversity Adjustment* can be difficult to accept, let alone welcome. For Jim Stovall, adversity appeared in his life at the tender age of just seventeen years.

Imagine having your life mapped out perfectly, only to have your dreams shredded by a life changing adversity. Jim Stovall's first *Life Purpose* was to play professional football for the Dallas Cowboys. He had the size, strength, and speed—he just needed to practice and continue to improve this football knowledge and skills. It seemed as if nothing could interrupt those plans—but a routine physical examination for football players introduced him to an *Adversity Adjustment* that would defeat most.

It didn't defeat Jim Stovall. In his book, *The Gift of Giving,* Jim recalled how he sat in an exam room for an agonizing amount of time. One doctor after another examined him, repeatedly shining lights into his eyes, and running tests. After a long wait, he was ushered into another room and given news that shattered his first *Life Purpose* dream of becoming an NFL football player.

Jim was going blind. He had a rare case of macular degeneration, and nothing could be done to stop it.

Shock and horror set in. Rather than starting a prestigious college football career, Jim moved into a small room in the back of his parent's home. He began attending Oral Roberts University, where his father worked as the Chief Financial Officer.

Without football, Jim switched his athletic goals to Olympic style weightlifting. By this time, his eyesight was fading. When fellow students signed up to read his textbooks to him, Jim chose to work solely with a student named Crystal, whom he later married.

As their friendship grew and they began dating, Crystal asked Jim what they would do when they finished college. He had three goals. He wanted to start a business and become a millionaire, write a book that would become a movie, and donate a million dollars to a cause he felt passionate about.

Those goals remained in his mind, but as graduation drew nearer, Jim realized he didn't know how to make them a reality. While his friends received job offers, no one wanted to hire a blind man. Starting his own business was his best option. When he announced his intention, his father directed him to Lee Braxton, who worked in the office next to his.

Lee Braxton was a disciple of Napoleon Hill's work and one of Dr. Hill's best friends. Although he appeared gruff and cranky, he became Jim's coach.

By this time, Jim could barely read, but Lee Braxton assigned him to read Dr. Hill's book, *Think and Grow Rich*. After reading the book, Mr. Braxton met with him, asked him a question, and quickly told him to read it again. This happened again on the second visit. On the third visit, they started their discussions based on the principles of the book and how to help Jim find his way. This included deep conversations about *Adversity Adjustment*—how to find the seed of a greater benefit in Jim's blindness. Rather than complaining, Jim was instructed to find the unique opportunities that being blind presented.

As Jim pondered the concept of equal or greater benefits, he noticed that many other people had their lives disrupted by blindness. They couldn't even watch television because television was designed for people who could see.

This sparked his first Big Idea: why not create a television network for the blind?

The Narrative Television Network was born. Through this business, Jim became a multi-millionaire. The Narrative Television Network now provides television services to 13 million people in the United States.

Because Jim learned to welcome *Adversity Adjustments,* he reached all the goals he had discussed with Crystal. He writes several columns and has published more than 40 books. Eight of his books have been produced into featured films. He and Crystal donated more than a million dollars to start a business incubator at Oral Roberts University.

Jim Stovall now speaks publicly. He teaches people that their adversities can become their biggest blessings. As devastating as it was, even going blind had its benefits. His difficulties provided him with opportunities to reach his goals and *Life Purpose*, and much more.

That goes for every person we've talked about in this book.

Britnie Turner found the seed of greater benefit when she was homeless, living in her car. Although she had no money, she had time to read, study, and practice what she learned. This experience gave her the specialized skills she needed to become successful.

Misty Copeland had a difficult beginning and family life. All the odds were against her. She found the seed of greater benefit as she embraced her athletic body, her desire to dance, and the people who supported her. She believed that she was going to be a ballerina, and she became one.

S. Truett Cathy faced financial ruin several times. His first business was too small to make the profit he needed. His second business burned to the ground. Even his third business fell through, but these *Adversity Adjustments* gave him the wisdom and the knowledge he needed to create the Chick-Fil-A success story.

Jeff Bezos struggled, first selling books out of his garage. The steep learning curve eventually showed him how to turn a profit, selling anything he wanted online. Amazon.com was born, and Jeff Bezos became one of the richest men in the world.

And then there's me.

As a young man, anger and bitterness directed my life. I thought the job of a dishwasher at Farrell's Ice Cream Parlour and Restaurant would be the most insignificant experience of my life. Then I met Mr. Farrell, and he introduced me to the book, *Think & Grow Rich*, by Dr. Napoleon Hill. Without a doubt, Mr. Farrell's interest in me was one of the most significant experiences of my life.

Mr. Farrell's mentorship and introduction to the work of Dr. Hill taught me to find the seeds of greater benefits within every adversity I was blessed with. I embraced my job at Farrell's and accepted restaurant work as the perfect chance to start my success journey.

The more I learned, the stronger my *Positive-State-of-Mind* became—and the easier it was to grow within the company. I learned how to become a leader and how to coach and mentor others to live up to their full potential. I became both a team player and a business leader, and I grew personally as well as financially. I obtained a *Success Mindset*.

Today, I own several businesses. The bitterness I felt as a young man has vanished. It's been replaced with enduring hope, gratitude, and compassion for life. I have learned to welcome the *Adversity Adjustment* process, because I know I will find greater benefits, every time. As I find those hidden opportunities, I continue to improve both my own life and the lives of others, all around the world.

I have learned that what seems like failure is only temporary unless I accept it as permanent. Success becomes inevitable when you believe it is inevitable and do the work to make it happen.

If you're still not sure you can embrace *Adversity Adjustment,* consider the positives that can come from what most consider a negative situation:

- **Adversity can show you where you need to adjust**—and how to do it. With this knowledge, you can replace bad habits with good ones.
- **Illness gives you the opportunity to change your lifestyle** and sometimes help other people change theirs.
- **Poor health and trauma can shift your perspective**. Sometimes, it's exactly what you need because it gives you compassion for other people who suffer the same way.
- **Adversity can humble you**. When your arrogance is challenged, the roadblocks to harmonious relationships are removed. This helps you develop a *Pleasing Personality* and improves all your relationships.
- **Challenging work relationships are improved**. This prepares the way for better, more harmonious Teamwork, where you and your team can achieve the *Genius Zone*.
- **Difficult situations give you the opportunity to take inventory of your strengths and weaknesses**. This can lead to the development of a better *Specialized Talent Team* to help you reach your goals, objectives, or *Life Purpose*.
- **Adversity is sometimes associated with grief and sorrow.** Those strong emotions can have a refining impact on you, deepening your ability to connect to *Infinite Intelligence*. As you seek consolation this way, you become more self-reliant, more self-assured, and more resourceful.

- **Adversity can cause a shift in what you consider as true wealth, which could change your life.** This happened for Britnie Turner when she was directed away from missionary work and into the real estate business to achieve her *Life Purpose* of helping others find their way.
- **If you are determined to overcome your challenges**, you develop a stronger willpower. Your *Self-Discipline* and confidence skyrocket.

Adversity Adjustment means turning adversity to your favor, and there are many ways you can do it. This is often an internal challenge, because you may not always be in control of the outer effects of adversity. Sometimes, relationships fall apart, reputations are damaged, or material goods are lost. You control the situation as you control your own reaction to it, experience the process of *Adversity Adjustment*, and profit by it.

When you experience emotional adversity and adjust to it without feeling like your inner soul is suffocated, you have become a master at *Adversity Adjustment*. This can happen in every area of life—this is how the world's greatest musicians, athletes, artists, leaders, and other geniuses are developed. Tragedy becomes a creative force when you embrace it, find the seed of greater benefit, and use it to refine yourself and your life.

Sometimes, adversity requires a change in your *Faith-Based Actions*. Sometimes, it results in completely adjusting your *Life Purpose*. As you embrace the lessons of *Adversity Adjustment*, you will discover they not only heal your heart wounds, but they can also be transformed into any form of creative effort you desire—and this could change everything in your life.

One of the benefits of *Adversity Adjustment* is that it combines immense individual achievement with humility. Success without humility isn't true success. It's just an empty

> **TAKEAWAYS**
>
> Those who accept and even welcome **Adversity Adjustment** increase their **Self-Discipline** and their humility, so they can see opportunities in every adjustment. **Adversity Adjustments become stepping stones to success.**

People who welcome adversity plan better, execute *Faith-Based Actions* better, and develop a stronger *Pleasing Personality*.

achievement that proves temporary and unsatisfying. You notice this most in people who become successful quickly, without experiencing adversity. They aren't happy, and their successes don't last.

Those who accept and even welcome *Adversity Adjustment* increase their *Self-Discipline* and their humility, so they can see opportunities in every adjustment. *Adversity Adjustments* become stepping stones to success. People who welcome adversity plan better, execute *Faith-Based Actions* better, and develop a stronger *Pleasing Personality*. The results are true success and everlasting happiness.

You can find evidence of this in every walk of life. Most often, individual success is in exact proportion to the scope of the *Adversity Adjustment* they have experienced and mastered.

This always circles back to achieving and maintaining a *Positive-State-of-Mind*.

As you face *Adversity Adjustment,* when you maintain a positive thought setting, you are likely to *Live Ready*®. You might endure some down moments and difficult circumstances, but if you refuse to surrender to the illusion of adversity, you will rise to higher and higher levels of achievement.

Maintaining a *Positive-State-of-Mind* allows you to recognize that adversity is just a temporary condition. The adjustment process is key to resolving all types of personal difficulties. A *Positive Mindset* is so important that it has been integrated into every chapter of this book and woven through every *Live Ready*® principle.

A *Positive-State-of-Mind* has the power to activate the Law of Attraction, so that you attract success as surely as a magnet attracts metal. As you adjust to adversity, you transform the illusion of defeat into an asset. You find the greater benefit, seize the opportunities presented to you, take *Faith-Based Actions,* and grow into a stronger version of yourself.

Adversity Adjustment demonstrates that faith and a *Positive-State-of-Mind* go hand in hand. Faith is the greatest power available to humanity because it pushes you to act, and a positive mindset is always behind it. Similarly, the faith to act is always behind your ability to *Pivot to Positive*®.

Both faith and a positive mindset are completely free. No matter what your position is in life, every time you face adversity, you can use these principles to help you master the *Adversity Adjustment* rule.

The best time to deal with adversity is before it occurs. To get the most out of *Adversity Adjustment,* you must embrace all the other *Live Ready*® principles in this book. These principles lay the foundation for you to see the seed of greater benefit every time you face adversity—and they always prepare you for the future, so that when you're faced with adversity, you can quickly pivot to a *Positive-State-of-Mind.*

Remember—adversity is not final unless it is accepted as final. The highest levels of success are achieved through *Adversity Adjustments,* which allow you to see opportunities for growth. Adversity tempers your nature so that you can be both successful and humble, and it allows you to use every challenge as a stepping stone to greater achievements. When you embrace the hope that *Adversity Adjustment* provides, you are strengthening your strategy. You're moving from the *Rhythm of Success* to the *Habit of Success*—and you're *Living Ready.*

Summary:

Adversity is not failure unless you accept it as so. It is merely an opportunity to adjust your course. *Adversity Adjustments* happen when you use adversity to simply pause, adjust your plan, and move forward.

Adversity Adjustment is the pivot point within the *Live Ready*® *principles of success.* This critical principle shows you how to remove limitations that are seeded into your subconscious as the result of believing adversity is failure. Adversity is not final unless you accept it as final. Every form of adversity brings with it the seed of a greater benefit—but you must learn to look for it.

Everyone confronts adversity. Truly great people welcome the *Adversity Adjustment* process and use it as a steppingstone to the highest levels of success.

**Access QR code
or at eleadertech.com/AAC**

"*Take care of your mind, your body will thank you. Take care of your body, your mind will thank you.*"

— DEBBIE HAMPTON

CHAPTER EIGHT

Sound Health

THINK BACK TO THE CLASSIC STORIES YOU READ AS A child and why you enjoyed them. Was it the pictures, a favorite character, or a saying you liked to repeat? Many times, those stories were trying to teach us something, even though we may not have fully understood it at the time.

One example is "The Little Engine That Could," which introduces one of the biggest secrets to success. In this story, several trains have the opportunity to pull the stranded cars filled with toys and treats over the mountain, and they all refuse. Yet an unlikely engine does because she thinks she can.

So why am I taking us on this walk down memory lane? Because the power of our thoughts can drive us to achieve *Sound Health*, often the most neglected *Live Ready*® principle. When thought drives action, our brain will gravitate to positive or negative solutions, depending on what imaginary outcome already exists within our mind. There is no such thing as neutral, because positive and negative cannot exist at the same time, so our brain has to choose.

Developing a *Happiness Consciousness* doesn't mean always walking around with a smile on your face. It's much more than that. We must look for all the ways *Sound Health* can be achieved and execute those health actions. You have to reprogram your brain to default to attracting positive health action thoughts and then act upon them. If you have an *unhappy consciousness* you will find it very difficult—if not impossible—to achieve *Sound Health*.

Sound Health just may be the most neglected *Live Ready*® principle. In this chapter you will learn that you cannot separate your body from your mind, for they are one. Anything that affects the health and energy of your mind will affect your body. And anything that affects the health and energy of your body will affect your mind. This truth is critical for the obtainment of *Sound Health*.

Without a *Positive-State-of-Mind* thought setting, the obtainment of *Sound Health* will prove to be impossible. Without *Sound Health*, achieving a *Positive-State-of-Mind* will also prove to be difficult.

The *Live Ready*® principles require the control and active application of a *Positive-State-of-Mind* setting. Your body is the temple in which your mind resides, and the mind-body combination allows your mind to execute its directives.

Neglecting *Sound Health* most often causes a loss of desire and the ability to execute the *Faith-based Actions* required to achieve your goals, objectives, or *Life Purpose*.

Sound Health starts with your thoughts. Consider the *Brain Model's Positive-State-Mind* benefits covered in previous chapters. A *Positive-State-of-Mind* is vital for the achievement of *Sound Health*. Maintaining a *Success Mindset* creates a *Happiness Consciousness*, optimizing your immune system to protect your body from diseases.

A *Negative-State-of-Mind* creates an *unhappiness consciousness* of fear and anxiety, which are destructive forces to your mind. A small amount of fear is normal. It mobilizes your body functions to defend against threats—to instantly prepare you to fight or run. But the defense mechanism of fear was not intended to be your controlling thought. To develop a *Happiness Consciousness* that can live comfortably with the everyday stresses of day-to-day life, one must replace a *Negative-State-of-Mind* thought setting of fear and anxiety with a *Positive-State-of-Mind*

TAKEAWAYS

If our health thoughts are organized, developed, believed, and used, our **subconscious will try and find a way to make them a reality.**

A *Positive-State-of-Mind* creates *Sound Health* and a *Negative-State-of-Mind* creates poor health.

thought setting of joy and faith, as taught throughout this entire book.

Remember, positive attracts positive and negative attracts negative. Your subconscious mind will validate whatever health thoughts your conscious mind and imagination send it. Thoughts are powerful. If our health thoughts are organized, developed, believed, and used, our subconscious will try and find a way to make them a reality. One of the greatest gifts to humankind starts with thought. A *Positive-State-of-Mind* creates *Sound Health* and a *Negative-State-of-Mind* creates poor health.

To best illustrate the power of *Sound Health*, I would like to share the Dr. José Antonio Calzada Story.

The Healer

Most people do not consider the idea of a *Life Purpose* until after their teenage years. Those that do merely wonder about how they are going to earn a living, and that is not a *Life Purpose*.

This was never the case with Dr. José Antonio Calzada. Dr. Calzada discovered his *Life Purpose* at the young age of eight years. Seeing people experience the trauma and sadness of an illness troubled him as a young boy. He often wondered how he could prevent people from getting sick. Even as a child, he felt motivated to dedicate his life to the wellness of others.

Imagine a young boy, playing with the family dogs in a loving, comfortable home in Acapulco, Mexico. José attended private Catholic schools and learned to play the guitar, but his real interest always came back to the wellness of the people and animals around him. When he saw that the people in his life, his family pets, and other animals weren't feeling well, he wanted to help.

The air in Acapulco was humid. Because of the climate, he and other children often came down with tonsilitis and had to go to the doctor's office. This usually included painful injections. He thought there had to be a cure that did not include the need for shots.

This was his first Big Idea, which turned into his *Life Purpose*—to find ways to help prevent disease and simply stay well. He started reading books on plants and herbs and what they could do to help treat specific ailments. Then, he started experimenting. He learned he could use chamomile for stomach aches and aloe vera for burns. When his dogs were sick, he cooked certain plants, fed them to his dogs, and watched his pets get well again. By the time he was ten years old, he was already beginning to tell people which plants to use, why they should use them, and how to prepare them as a remedy.

Like many boys, his hobbies were wide and varied. As a teenager, José was interested in both architecture and medicine. For a while, he even considered architecture as a career—but *Infinite Intelligence* whispered to his soul, reminding him of his childhood desires to help heal others. This led him back to the path of preventive medicine.

At that point, his *Life Purpose* developed into a *Career Purpose:* he was going to be a doctor and help people avoid the painful, uncomfortable treatments that accompany diseases.

The young José Calzada began studying at the college of medicine in Toluca, Mexico. While he was there, he became good friends with a young man who worked at the local Red Cross. His desire to learn as much as he could burned in his heart, mind, and soul. He asked his friend if he could come to the Red Cross to observe the work they did.

José Calzada began working at the Red Cross on weekends, investigating the skills and talents used there to assist people in need. At that time, he also played his guitar in a band. He composed songs and shared them with those who came to listen to his musical talent—which gave him great joy.

He considered becoming a musician, but working at the Red Cross inspired him to stay true to his *Life Purpose* of helping people achieve *Sound Health*. He again heard the whisper of *Infinite Intelligence*, saying "You belong here." Once and for all, he rededicated himself to his medical studies and graduated as a general practitioner medical doctor.

His university medical training took seven years, from the age of 17 until he was 24. This included two years of internship at a hospital. Once he graduated, he was obligated by law to give one year of medical service free of charge.

His goal was to finish his year of service and then specialize in one area of medicine. In Mexico, becoming specialized required passing a very difficult test, as well as laser-focused continued education and training. Dr. Calzada started his medical career working in an emergency room in Acapulco. This experience increased his skills as a care provider, which he hoped would prepare him to select a specialization.

One evening, an American woman of about 80 years of age was admitted to the emergency room. Dr. Calzada treated her, and she got well. To show her gratitude, she came back a week later and gave him a book as a gift.

Dr. Calzada's natural curiosity and burning desire to learn more kicked in, and he quickly read the book. It featured treatments like chelation therapy with the use of EDTA, colonics, lymphatic massage, and other techniques to heal people suffering from cancer and other chronic diseases. The content inspired him to learn more.

These treatments were already being offered in Mexico, Europe, Asia, and other parts of the world. The book stirred Dr. Calzada's emotions. He could see how these techniques could benefit his own patients. He had to find a way to learn more.

His curiosity and desire to learn caused him to become a sending and receiving station for *Infinite Intelligence,* making it easier to find his answers. His reticular activating system (RAS) went to work, and it didn't take long before opportunities began to appear.

While he was working in the hospital's emergency room, his grandfather's brother had a heart attack. Dr. Calzada treated him. Afterwards, a visiting family member saw the book Dr. Calzada had been reading—and he recognized it.

This family member worked in Tijuana, near Rosarito, where the hospital featured in the book was located. He offered to introduce Dr. Calzada to the doctors that worked there. Dr. Calzada was delighted to accept. He flew to Tijuana, eager to learn more.

The team of doctors at the hospital appreciated Dr. Calzada's enthusiasm for their treatments, and they were interested in Dr. Calzada's experience as an emergency room doctor. They needed a skilled emergency doctor to help them treat patients with cancer and other chronic diseases.

His inquisitiveness paid off. At the age of 25, he was offered a position with this hospital. He began studying these new treatments, while at the same time, providing the emergency care the hospital needed. Dr. Calzada learned about colonics, chelation therapy, and other techniques, and he joined the American College in Advance of Medicine.

There was another hospital nearby where famous people from around the world came for wellness and longevity care. This hospital featured medical interventions designed by a brilliant Swiss scientist, Dr. Paul Niehans, who had developed some of the first cellular and longevity therapy treatments. Although Dr. Niehans passed away in 1971, his renowned cellular therapy and innovative methods for arresting the aging process continued to flourish. They were highlighted at this hospital, and Dr. Calzada was immediately interested in them. He decided to visit and see if there might be an opportunity to learn more about them.

There was. After his visit, Dr. Calzada was offered a part time position, scheduled around his work at the Rosarito Wellness Center. He accepted, and the doctors there began teaching him Dr. Niehans' cellular therapy, along with the new techniques they discovered.

Dr. Calzada began experimenting and integrating his knowledge to improve the cellular treatments. Soon, he began using this cellular therapy with his patients at the Rosarito Wellness Center, and the results were remarkable. A doctor came from Germany seeking his help to heal his sciatic nerve pain issues. This doctor was so impressed with Dr. Calzada's work that he offered to teach him a new type of cellular therapy. Over time, Dr. Calzada became known as an expert in cellular therapy, chelation therapy, colonics, and a host of other alternative techniques that focus on creating *Sound Health*. He was more of a specialist than he ever would have been if he had followed the traditional medical path—and he had specialized in a way that allowed him to prevent illness.

In 1991, he decided to open his own office. He opened a very small clinic in Tijuana. His practice started to grow and as it did, he offered more techniques and therapies. He quickly gained a reputation as a doctor who could help when traditional medical treatments could not. His practice began to attract patients from California, Utah, and other places throughout the western United States.

One day, when Dr. Calzada was working alone in his office, he heard a knock on the door. He opened the door and faced a desperate father—Floyd Weston—who had heard of Dr. Calzada's work and had come all the way from Utah to see him.

Floyd Weston's adult daughter was a diabetic and was required to take insulin shots. Over time, she had become allergic to insulin. Without the insulin shots, she would die, and her seven small children would be motherless. He begged Dr. Calzada for his help, and Dr. Calzada quickly agreed.

During the next two weeks, Floyd Weston's daughter visited Dr. Calzada's office every day. She had IV treatments, and Dr. Calzada began using some homeopathic remedies on her, as well. At the end of the second week, her allergies had disappeared, and her body was accepting the insulin injections again.

Floyd Weston was a bishop of the Church of Jesus Christ of Latter-day Saints. He was overcome with emotion and gratitude, and he insisted that Dr. Calzada visit him in Utah. When Dr. Calzada came, Mr. Weston introduced him to everyone in his congregation and told them his daughter's story.

Dr. Calzada explained the treatments he offered to help his patients achieve *Sound Health*. At the end of the visit, he returned to Mexico. His advice for developing wellness was well-received, and his reputation spread. He became known for successfully treating patients who had been given little to no hope. More and more people began coming to Dr. Calzada, seeking answers for their ailments.

In time, Dr. Calzada was able to buy some land and build a state-of-the-art clinic in Tijuana. He flew around the world, visiting clinics to continue his education. This included spending time at the hospitals in the Black Forest region of Germany, where he learned even more about cellular therapy treatment. He also became certified in homeopathy. Dr. Calzada founded the BioAdvanced Medical Center, which has become one of the premier wellness clinics in the Americas.

I personally met Dr. Calzada in the early 1990s, when I accompanied a dear friend to Mexico to seek treatment for his terminal cancer. At that time, Dr. Calzada was working in his small, rented office, with only one nurse to assist him. I believed this first chance meeting would be insignificant. I didn't realize at the time that I had crossed paths with someone who would change my life.

My friend was referred to Dr. Calzada by Floyd Weston's son, who was his chiropractor. At that time, my friend had been diagnosed with stage four cancer, and had been told he had a life expectancy of only eight weeks. When Dr. Calzada examined him, he explained it was too late to cure the cancer, but he was confident that with treatments, he could extend my friend's life for two more years of good living. After that, the cancer would flare up again, and he would pass away.

My friend gladly accepted the treatments and promised to work hard to achieve the *Positive-State-of-Mind* that Dr. Calzada told him would be required. He lived well for another twenty-eight months before the cancer flared up, just as Dr. Calzada explained it would.

TAKEAWAYS

A *Positive-State-of-Mind* attracts positivity and wellness, while a *Negative-State-of-Mind* attracts negativity and illness.

Your *State-of-Mind* impacts your happiness, and your happiness impacts your health.

My friend passed away three months later. During his last weeks, he repeatedly told me and anyone else who would listen how thankful he was for the extra time he had with his family and friends.

I was in decent health, but after observing Dr. Calzada's incredible gift of healing, I wondered what he could do for me. When I asked him, Dr. Calzada told me he could treat aging as if it was a disease. His longevity treatments and cellular therapy could slow my aging process, so that I would only age two to three years for every ten years that I lived. I immediately began receiving treatments from him.

That was nearly twenty-nine years ago. I still visit Dr. Calzada's clinic three times a year, spending three or four days at his clinic during each visit. The results have been magical, and they have impacted my mind even more than my body.

Every time I've visited Dr. Calzada, he has focused on my emotions as much as my physical health. This is normal for him. I see him teaching the *Brain Model* to all his new patients, drawing it out on a white board. He tells them, "If you can't learn and believe in the power of your thoughts, then I can't help you. But if you learn this *Brain Model*, and how to create and maintain a *Positive-State-of-Mind*, then achieving *Sound Health* and wellness is very possible."

Dr. Calzada introduced me to the power of the *Brain Model*, and how to utilize it to achieve *Sound Health*. I expanded his version to include Dr. Hill's work, along with my own. The *Brain Model* has subsequently become a large part of my performance improvement practice. I have introduced the *Brain Model* to thousands of students. I feature it in all my work, and I included it in both of my books. It's essential for helping people understand the power of a

Positive-State-of-Mind and how to become the *Switch Master of Your Own Thought*® and *Pivot to Positive*® to *Live Ready*®.

Dr. Calzada teaches all his patients that *Sound Health* starts by understanding that thoughts are powerful. The brain can create a *Positive-State-of-Mind* so your body can optimize its immune system to protect and heal itself. It can also create a *Negative-State-of-Mind*, where your immune system is redirected to battling stress, emotional strain, and tension. This prevents your body from being able to protect and heal itself. A *Positive-State-of-Mind* attracts positivity and wellness, while a *Negative-State-of-Mind* attracts negativity and illness.

This is essential to understand, because your *State-of-Mind* impacts your happiness, and your happiness impacts your health.

Living in a *Negative-State-of-Mind* leads you to do things that could hurt or destroy you. It contributes to bad choices in what and how you eat, the excessive use of alcohol or tobacco, the inappropriate use of prescription drugs, or even the use of illegal drugs. It leads you to disregard personal and professional relationships, set aside exercise, and develop other bad habits that harm your body, your mind, and your soul.

When you're happy, you gain respect for the temple in which your soul resides. You understand that you're a mind-body, and you want to get the most out of the mind-body experience. Your behaviors reflect that, and you are naturally drawn to healthy habits that promote wellness.

What you do to your mind, you do to your body, and what you do to your body, you do to your mind. They are one. Dr. Calzada discovered that happiness helps you build healthy habits, but even more importantly, it helps you keep your immune system strong. When you're in a *Happiness Consciousness*, your immune system connects with your mind-body and protects it.

Once I understood this, I became a disciple of Dr. Calzada's wellness guidance,

TAKEAWAYS

When you're in a **Happiness Consciousness,** your immune system connects with your mind-body and protects it.

When you're happy, you gain respect for the temple in which your soul resides.

just as I had earlier become a disciple of Dr. Napoleon Hill's *Science of Success* principles. Their *Sound Health* teachings are intertwined. You must focus on a *Positive-State-of-Mind* and happiness to achieve *Sound Health* and *Live Ready*®.

Dr. Calzada understands that health and happiness are related. Happiness is a choice you make when you determine to live in a *Positive-State-of-Mind*. You are the only person who can make that choice for yourself.

One visit, as I waited for my appointment, I sat next to a man from Nebraska. The man was crying, because his wife and business partner had liver cancer and had been told she was terminally ill. I tried to reassure him by telling him she wasn't dead yet, and I was certain Dr. Calzada could help her.

Three years later, as I waited for Dr. Calzada to arrive, one of his nurses collapsed. A lady in the waiting room helped me get the nurse off the floor and onto a table. Dr. Calzada arrived and immediately treated her. As I looked at the woman who helped me, I recognized her—she was the lady from Nebraska, still alive, healthy, and happier than ever.

Dr. Calzada has helped thousands of people change the quality of their lives by switching out their fear for happiness. He has the gift of helping people find the seed of greater benefit even in their illness.

Being ill is about more than just being sick. It's about finding the power to ascend to a *Happiness Consciousness*. As you heal—really heal—you end the inner sadness and become positive and happy. You begin to look at the person in the mirror differently, and you start to love yourself. When you do, you set yourself up to *Live Ready*®.

Dr. Calzada believes there's a unique satisfaction that comes from doing the right things to bless other people. When you do, you're living with your soul and your heart. You're not just motivated by money—you're motivated by the joy of giving. You're delighted by the chance of becoming happy yourself and thrilled with the idea of becoming an instrument in the hands of *Infinite Intelligence*. In this state, your body could last for more than 100 years, and you could be active and happy the entire time.

Happiness leads to wellness.

Unfortunately, today's society is packed with people who are unhappy and unhealthy. Some of these people become greedy, self-centered *drifters* who want something for nothing. Many others see themselves as victims, unable to take control of their lives and shift to a *Positive-State-of-Mind*. Their limited, unhappy views of themselves cause their immune systems to disconnect from their mind-bodies, so they are less protected from disease.

Happiness is the first step to correcting that trend, because it eliminates destructive behaviors. Feelings of happiness lead you to find your *Life Purpose* and to value yourself. You recognize that your body is a temple, and you have the privilege of caring for it.

Dr. Calzada teaches that when you're happy, your body tells you exactly what you need to do to keep it healthy. You sleep well, exercise, and eat well almost automatically. You give and receive love easily, and you become a sending and receiving station for *Infinite Intelligence*. This allows you to hear whispers of truth the same way Dr. Calzada did when he decided to study medicine. Happiness and *Living Ready* are connected to each other.

Dr. Calzada wants people to know they can cure themselves, simply by being authentically happy and doing things for the good of other people. It's important to experience and enjoy every second of life.

It took me a long time to figure this out, but it finally dawned on me that I cannot make anyone else happy. If I make myself

TAKEAWAYS

Feelings of happiness lead you to find your *Life Purpose* and to value yourself. You recognize that your body is a temple, and you have the privilege of caring for it.

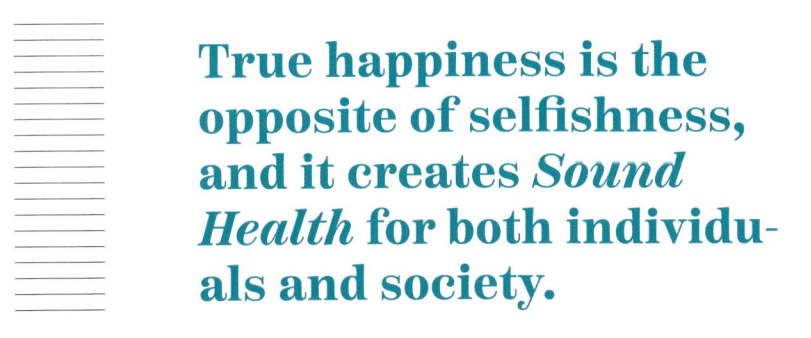

> **True happiness is the opposite of selfishness, and it creates *Sound Health* for both individuals and society.**

happy, that allows me to give more freely and be a better person to others, so happiness can spread. True happiness is the opposite of selfishness, and it creates *Sound Health* for both individuals and society.

For these reasons, I visit Dr. Calzada three times a year to achieve and maintain *Sound Health*. These reasons are also why I share the *Brain Model* with as many people as I can. If they can learn to understand the *Brain Model*, they will realize they're in control of their own happiness, and they can shift into a *Success Mindset* to get what they could and should have.

The interesting thing about the connection between happiness and wellness is that it extends beyond health. It influences education, developing your skills and talent, and making life better for everyone you interact with. It has the potential to strengthen our economy, so we could invest in medical care, wellness care, and education for everyone who desires to improve themselves. When people are happy and healthy, they develop their talent and skills to achieve their *Life Purpose* and *Live Ready*®.

Fear and anxiety produce an *unhappiness consciousness* that leads to serious instability and eventually produces its counterpart in the body in poor health. There are many wellness experts that believe many physical ailments are related to a negative mindset or *unhappiness consciousness*.

The fear of getting sick is destructive. This anxiety causes many people to believe that they are ill or are going to become ill. And, as you recall from the *Brain Model* discussions of the subconscious mind, *be careful of what you think because you just might get it*.

The *Readiness Mindset* principle greatly affects *Sound Health*. Going the Extra Mile, Personal Initiative, Self-Discipline, Controlled Attention, Controlled Enthusiasm, Accurate Thought, and Creative Vision elevate you to a *Happiness Consciousness,* which can create a high likelihood of achieving *Sound Health* and *Living Ready*.

Two of the greatest destructive forces in the mind are fear and its close partner, anxiety. They kill enthusiasm, destroy faith, blind vision, block creative effort and destroy harmony and peace of mind—all the qualities necessary for achieving a *Happiness Consciousness*. Pivoting a *Negative-State-of-Mind* to a *Positive-State-of-Mind* aids in the development of bodily resistance against disease.

Proper nutrition is important, too. Essential nutrients from food help create *Sound Health* by keeping the immune system strong. They are also vital to the biochemical processes that support a *Success Mindset.*

Our bodies need a wide variety of nutrients. Carbohydrates and fats help provide energy, while protein provides the building blocks for our body tissues. Vitamins and minerals have crucial roles in how our cells and body tissues function.

Water is essential, too. It affects the function of every system in your body. Your mind-body can go weeks without food, but only a few days without water. Water keeps you hydrated, boosts your metabolism, and encourages cell rejuvenation. Even mild dehydration can impair your concentration and physical performance.

To get the right amount of nutrients, we have to eat the right kinds of foods, in the proper amounts for our bodies. Doctors, dieticians, fitness trainers, health coaches, and a variety of other professionals often differ on their recommendations for what to eat and when to eat. Remember, as you come to love and appreciate your body, it will let you know which nutrients you need and when you need them.

As a general rule, mind-bodies function best when people eat a well-balanced diet, built around fresh, nutrient-dense foods.

TAKEAWAYS

Fear and anxiety produce an unhappiness consciousness that leads to serious instability and eventually produces its counterpart in the body in poor health.

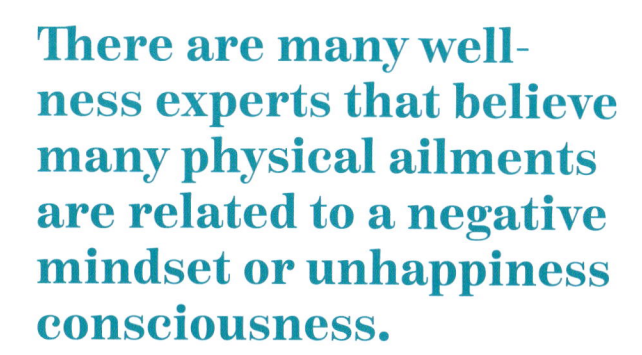

> **There are many wellness experts that believe many physical ailments are related to a negative mindset or unhappiness consciousness.**

As you build your personal eating plan around what your mind-body requires, consider the following suggestions:

- **Try to base your meals around fresh vegetables**. They provide essential vitamins, minerals, and other chemicals that develop health on a cellular level. They're also packed with fiber.
- **Listen to your body** concerning how much energy you should get from carbohydrates, proteins, and fats. Experiment and find a ratio that works for you.
- **Be modest** in your carbohydrate intake.
- When you eat carbs, **consider focusing on whole grains and beans**. They provide protein, vitamins, and minerals. The fiber in whole grains and beans could help improve your digestive tract, too. This is important because your gut health can impact your mood, helping you maintain a Positive-State-of-Mind.
- **Remember to eat enough protein** to provide your body with all the building blocks it needs. Protein is found abundantly in meats, fish, dairy, beans, nuts, and seeds.
- **Eat fermented foods once in a while.** Fermented foods like yogurt, kimchi, and sauerkraut provide essential probiotics that help keep your digestive tract healthy and your mood happy.

- **Choose simple, natural foods**—leave processed foods and sugary treats to people who aren't interested in *Sound Health*.
- **Consult with your doctor** about taking vitamins or other supplements to help you get all the nutrients you need.

One of the simplest ways of selecting foods is to seek variety. The more varied and colorful your foods are, the higher the probability that you are getting the nutrients your body needs.

If you can, reduce stressful situations around mealtimes. The more relaxed you are, the easier it will be to digest your food. Keep conversations pleasant. If you're eating alone, focus on your food. Notice how many times you chew, what the food looks like, and how it tastes. This simple mindful eating practice develops feelings of gratitude, which helps keep you in a *Success Mindset*.

Just as your body can guide you to the proper nutrition plan for you, it can guide you to other *Sound Health* practices. Pay attention to the needs of your mind-body as you shift into your daily to-do list, including getting enough sleep, balancing work and play, and exercising.

Physical activity and exercise can have immediate and long-term health benefits. Proper exercise can reduce stress, regulate weight, boost the immune system, and improve sleep. Regular exercise can improve your health and reduce the risk of developing diseases like type 2 diabetes, cancer, and cardiovascular disease.

As you experiment with different types of physical activity, pay attention to the types of exercise that feel fun to you. Fun physical activities boost your happiness levels, releasing the DOSE chemicals we discussed in the *Brain Model* section of this book. They also reduce stress, preparing you for relaxation practices that support your *Success Mindset*.

Relaxation is important for maintaining *Sound Health* and well-being. Relaxation improves your mental health and gives your body a chance to take a break. It releases

TAKEAWAYS

Your body needs time to rebuild and revitalize itself to prepare for the next day. It is foolish to cut your sleep time. Somewhere between six and eight hours is all that is required.

Eat right, think right, sleep right, and play right to achieve Sound Health and get what you want.

muscle tension, lowers your blood pressure, and improves your digestion. Choose a type of relaxation that you enjoy, something that gives you satisfaction and relaxes both your body and your mind. This helps prepare you for deep, restful sleep at the end of the day.

Sleep is essential for the attainment of *Sound Health*. It is just as important as healthy eating and exercise. During sleep, your body rebuilds muscle and cleans away harmful plaques and wastes that are produced in the brain. Wounds heal, and body chemicals are balanced. These are vital processes that keep your mind-body running properly.

When you sleep, your mind processes and responds to important emotions and experiences from the day, committing them to memory. Sleep is also essential to regulating your emotions. Studies have found that being sleep-deprived for just one night can increase your emotional response to negative feelings by 60%.

Good sleep can even maximize problem-solving skills and enhance memory. Longer sleep has been shown to improve many aspects of physical performance.

Your body needs time to rebuild and revitalize itself to prepare for the next day. It is foolish to cut your sleep time. Somewhere between six and eight hours is all that is required.

Take a close look at your life. Have you developed a *Sound Health—Rhythm of Success*? Are you in balance? Most understand that there must be time set aside for work, but do you set aside time for the rhythm of relaxation? Are you balancing both physical and mental exercise? Are you properly feeding your body with proper nutrition, and are you properly feeding your mind with positive thoughts?

Eat right, think right, sleep right, and play right to achieve *Sound Health* and get what you want.

Summary:

The following steps, if applied daily, can help you achieve a *Positive Health Consciousness*.

1. **Shed Negativity** – The first step is to identify negativity in your day and get rid of it. Avoid participating in gossip and negative conversations. Make a conscious choice to not get offended by others. Reject self-pity and embrace self-reliance. Recognize bad habits and commit to abstaining from them for a month. In doing so, you build up the muscle memory of controlling your thoughts.
2. **Train Your Brain** – Once you've swept out the negative, make room for the positive. Find things you love to do, whether it be in the office or a hobby, and then devote time to doing it. Keep your mind busy doing positive things, then track those things daily and express gratitude for the rewards.
3. **Focus Outward** – Focusing on others builds empathy and relationships. Helping others find solutions to their problems oftentimes leads to a solution in your own life and health. Look for the good in others and find at least one thing to like in every person.
4. **Improve Yourself** – Once you rely on internal validation of your worthiness of *Sound Health*, you can build on that externally. Improving yourself is much easier when it comes from a *Happiness Consciousness*, rather than fear or self-doubt of an undesirable outcome.
5. **Healthy Body, Healthy Mind** – Getting enough sleep, eating a balanced diet, exercising, and taking time for relaxation protects against stress, anxiety, and depression. A healthy body creates a

healthy mind. Aging does not mean loss of health if you don't fear getting older. Embrace the wisdom that is earned over time.

Every person has the ability to pivot their mind to a *Positive-State-of-Mind* to achieve *Sound Health*—and it's never too late to start. You do not have to be a victim of your circumstances. You can choose to battle those circumstances through the power of your own thoughts. Just be like that little engine from your childhood and start with thinking you can!

Sound Health *challenge*

**Access QR code
or at eleadertech.com/SHC**

> "Tell me how you use your spare time and how you spend your money, and I will tell you where and what you will be in ten years from now."

— NAPOLEON HILL

CHAPTER NINE

Optimizing Time and Money

IF YOU ARE NOT WHERE YOU WANT TO BE, THERE IS A REAson. Most likely, it has something to do with the way you utilize your *Time* and *Money*.

Time squandered is time wasted that cannot be replaced, and no one has invented a way to make more time. *Money* squandered is money wasted and that money is lost forever—but you can make more money.

When most *Drifters* are challenged about their poor utilization of *Time* and *Money*, they will try to justify their wastefulness with excuses, but excuses will not bring back *Time* and *Money* that has been misspent.

When you *Live Ready*® you optimize the use of *Time* and *Money*. The *Living Ready* principle gives the word "utilization" a whole new meaning. It goes beyond the simple budgeting process and ensures that your *Time* and *Money* investments yield you the greatest results possible.

In this chapter you will learn to balance your use of *Time* in three major areas: *Sleep Time, Work Time,* and *Spare Time*. You will learn the art of spending *Money*, as well as saving it. Perhaps most importantly, you will learn the *Live Ready*® success formula: **Talent + Time + Money = Success.**

In Chapter Three, we discussed the value of *Talent*. The *Live Ready*® success formula includes *Talent* because no one person has all the *Talent* to achieve what they want by themselves. The development of a *Specialized Talent Team* allows you to get the required *Talent* to enter the *Genius Zone* to creatively utilize *Time* and *Money*.

Put simply, *Living Ready* is the optimization of *Talent, Time,* and *Money* so success becomes inevitable.

Mastering the *Optimizing Time and Money* principle, both personally and in business, creates self-confidence. Honesty and hard work alone are never enough to ensure success. When you *Live Ready*®, you naturally invest both *Time* and *Money* intelligently to achieve what you want.

If the *Optimizing Time and Money* principle is not mastered, the effectiveness of all the other *Live Ready*® principles will be greatly diminished, making it nearly impossible to achieve a *Success Mindset*.

Today, I am going to ask you to evaluate your *Time* and *Money* utilization. If you find you are wasting *Time* and or *Money*, you have a great *Adversity Adjustment* opportunity—so let's get started!

You have learned there are two types of people: The *Pure Non-Drifter* and the mild to severe *Drifter*.

The *Pure Non-Drifter* is a person who has a *Life Purpose,* along with detailed plans and actions to achieve it. The *Pure Non-Drifter* thinks their own thoughts and assumes full responsibility for them, whether they are right or wrong. These people have carefully selected their careers and are leaders in their chosen field. They express *Purpose* through action, and they follow the habit of *Going the Extra Mile*. Their *Personal Initiative* moves them forward. They are self-directed.

Pure Non-Drifters operate within the *Habit of Success*, controlling their thoughts and actions by utilizing *Self-Discipline*. They maintain a *Positive-State-of-Mind* and imagine only the things they want, and not the things they don't want. They have zero doubt. They support their *Purpose* and decisions with *Faith-Based Action*. This includes surrounding themselves with *Specialized Talent Teams* to help them carry out their *Purpose*. As they work toward their goals, they embrace *Adversity Adjustments,* recognizing their own weaknesses and finding ways to overcome them.

Because they are *Purpose*-driven, they also value their *Time* and *Money*. Using *Accurate Thought,* they plan and invest both *Time* and *Money* with laser-like focus to achieve their goals, objectives, or *Life Purpose*. Their *Success Mindset* and *Pleasing Personality* create a dynamic sense of presence and command.

Many *Pure Non-Drifters* are business leaders who are self-made. They learned to plan, organize, execute, and follow up to funnel *Time* and *Money* into *Faith-based Action*.

Pure Non-Drifters view email, text, and social media interactions during scheduled *Times Blocks* within their day. They manage technology. Technology does not manage them. They guard against losing their *Controlled Attention*.

Pure Non-Drifters hold themselves accountable for how they spend their resources. They make their *Time* and *Money* work for them, so they can rest peacefully at the end of their day.

People living without a pure *Success Mindset* are *Drifters*. They range from mild to severe.

Mild *Drifters* may understand how to *Pivot-to-Positive*®, but they don't maintain a *Positive-State-of-Mind* long enough to attain the *Habit of Success*. Severe *Drifters* are stuck in a *Negative-State-of-Mind*. They live in the *Negative Nuthouse,* always tormented by the whispers of Dr. Doubt.

Both mild and severe *Drifters* rely on others instead of themselves to lead. They accept the thoughts, ideas, and opinions of others easily, following the path of least resistance in all areas of their lives. Because they do not hold themselves accountable, they never learn from their mistakes—and they are caught in a cycle of repeated disappointments.

Drifters make no attempt to discipline or control their thoughts, so many of them never learn the power of sustained positive thinking. Their minds wander and Big Ideas float past them, never noticed. Achieving *Controlled Attention* is next to impossible for them.

In Napoleon Hill's fictional story *Outwitting the Devil,* the devil stated he feared nothing except that the world might sometimes produce a thinker who would use their own mind. He added that he controlled all *Drifters* who neglect to use their own minds—but the Adversary isn't the only individual who exploits the *Drifter*. *Drifters* can easily be taken advantage of by almost anyone who has a stronger opinion or influence.

The price *Drifters* pay is a heavy one. Consider this:

- **Drifters neglect their health because they pay more attention to material things than they do to their own mind-body.** Without *Self-Discipline*, they can never achieve *Sound Health* and the rewards that go with it. They waste their *Time* being unhealthy and they waste their *Money* seeking cures rather than prevention.
- **Drifters have trouble making and keeping strong family relationships.** They waste *Time* quarreling, nagging, and finding fault in the people closest to them, rather than creating a sense of harmony, loyalty, and unified *Purpose*.
- **Drifters can never enjoy the advantages of a Specialized Talent Team.** Their unpleasant personalities preclude them from developing true *Teamwork* in their careers, so they waste *Time and Money*.
- **Drifters don't have a Purpose to direct them**. *Drifters* are an odd combination of indifference, indecision, and confusion. Rather than being led by a *Purpose* or a labor of love, they are at the mercy of their circumstances—and they are often in a state of crisis. This wastes both *Time and Money*.

TAKEAWAYS

The way we use our time has an immense impact on how we earn, spend, and save money, so it is critical to invest *Time* properly.

Time Blocking is the key to the lock that prevents most people from *Living Ready*.

- **Drifters can't utilize Accurate Thought** to help guide their decisions for saving, spending, and making money.
- **Drifters lose their resources because they waste them.** Drifters view email, text, and social media interactions the moment they are received—which can be often. They are more interested in their Facebook "likes" than their "time" utilization. Technology manages them. They do not manage technology. They rarely have *Controlled Attention*.

If you suspect you have some *Drifter* tendencies, now is the time to make the necessary *Adversity Adjustments* and get back on course to optimize your *Time* and *Money*.

Most people have heard the phrase 'Time is Money.' The way we use our time has an immense impact on how we earn, spend, and save money, so it is critical to invest *Time* properly. *Time Blocking* is the key to the lock that prevents most people from *Living Ready*. Achieving eight hours of *Sleep Time* each day to rejuvenate your body and gain the energy to heighten your performance seems simple, but for many it is the weakest link to *Living Ready*.

Achieving this basic need can be a game changer.

Executing *Work Time* actions with *Controlled Attention* will ensure you get more done in eight-hours of *Work Time* than you previously did in twelve-hours.

Dedicating eight hours each day to *Spare Time* activities will strengthen your relationships. Effective spare time utilization is the backbone of all great achievement, for it creates a family/friends, faith, community, health, and financial wealth *happiness consciousness*.

A good example of *Time Blocking* your eight hours of *Spare Time* could include the following: one hour of meditation, two hours in the service of others, one hour for personal development, one hour for *Specialized Talent Team* activity, and three hours dedicated to recreation and family.

Use this example to create your own *happiness consciousness* through *Time Blocking* your *Spare Time*.

Due to your multiple life roles, you will always have requests for your *Time* coming at you from many directions. Your family/friends, faith, community, health, and financial wealth roles require your time. When you fail in one role it affects all the other life roles.

The key to achieving success and happiness seems to be simple—just live in balance. Have you ever met a person living in complete balance? Well, that just might be because there is no such thing as true balance. Consider this: on Amazon.com there are over 3,000 books offered on finding balance in your life.

For many people, work responsibilities seem to dominate their thoughts, clouding their effort to be mentally present in their other life roles. How do you stay *Purpose-driven* and find balance with so many demands on your time? The key to living in balance is to not be out of balance in any life role for very long. Never totally ignore a life role, for if you do, you will pay the penalty associated with it.

A *Success Mindset* relies on developing a balance in your family/friends, faith, community, health, and financial wealth life roles. Organizing your time into blocks of *Controlled Attention* in the activities associated with that role can boost your performance in all areas of your life.

A quick Google search of "productive work hours in an 8-hour workday" will offer you various studies stating the answer is only 3 hours. That means there is an opportunity—at minimum—to double work productivity.

TAKEAWAYS

Your family/friends, faith, community, health, and financial wealth roles require your time. **When you fail in one role it affects all the other life roles.**

> **The key to living in balance is to not be out of balance in any life role for very long.**

Optimizing the *Time Blocking* technique to execute your job role activities with excellence will ensure *work-worry* does not accompany you home. *Time Block* for work preparation, both at the beginning of the day and toward the end of your workday. Being properly prepared helps create a *Readiness Mindset,* so you can get the most out of your scheduled work *Time*. Your clarity, *Accurate Thinking*, and productivity will thank you for it.

Utilizing uninterrupted *Time Blocks* for the sole purpose of preparation will ensure all your work *Time Blocks* are optimized to their fullest. Most days, you will be able to depart work at your scheduled time, because all your work will be done. You will feel free and energized because you will have conquered work.

As you perfect your *Time Blocking* skills, you will begin to influence other people around you. You will train them to respect *Time*—your time.

Leaders: try placing a "Welcome" sign on your office door when you are inviting team members to your open *Time Block*—meaning it is open to anyone—no appointment is necessary. This *Time Block* should be scheduled during the same time each day whenever possible.

Flip the sign over to "Do Not Disturb" for *Time Blocks* requiring concentration. Of course, you must be available at any time if it is important enough to warrant an interruption in your *Controlled Attention*. Within weeks, everyone will respect your *Time Blocking* process, because they know you value *Time* and use it well. Your associates will start following your *Time Blocking* example. Your work culture will become so efficient that some days, you will become bored because there are no more fires to put out.

Optimizing your *Time* to gain *Controlled Attention* is the key to conquering work and achieving personal financial freedom.

When you fail to optimize your *Work Time* you will go home with work thoughts dominating your mind. And while you might be home, you are not mentally present. You're in that dark work cloud, and your family can feel your attention disconnection.

If this sounds like you, it's *Time* for an *Adversity Adjustment*!

It is equally important to evaluate how you invest *Time* in your family role. The truth is, if you spend thirty minutes a day with a family member—with no distraction—no text messages, no social media, no phone calls, or interruptions of any kind—your family relationships will flourish.

Turn your *Controlled Attention,* with a *Pleasing Personality,* toward the people that matter to you most—your family. *Time Block* thirty to sixty minutes, at least twice a week, with each of your family members. During that time, give them the gift of you—fully present—and you'll receive the gift of them in return.

Now let's shift to your *Sound Health* role. You can't develop *Sound Health* unless you have a *Time Block* for health. As you develop *Time Blocking* skills, you will find it easier to schedule *Time* for exercise, for relaxation, and for social activities that intrigue you and keep your mind-body healthy. None of these *Sound Health* practices will be overwhelming. In fact, because you break them into smaller *Time Blocks,* they will feel easy.

Your *Sound Health* practices might shift over the years, but the principle should remain the same. Small *Time Blocks,* even as short as two minutes, can have tremendous health benefits.

For example, when you get up in the morning, you brush your teeth—that's a very small block of time, but it is essential to your physical and mental well-being. Next, you might want to do 10-25 pushups, followed by 10-25 leg lifts. Through the rest of your morning routine, you could alternate a self-care activity with another set of 10-25 pushups and 10-25 abdominal exercises. Shortly it will become a morning ritual, just like making your bed or brushing your teeth.

These small *Time Blocks* can be combined with longer ones for full workouts, healthy sleep, and proper nutrition. Small *Time Blocks* can easily be woven into your daily routines, and they can overlap. There are a lot of things you can do in two-minute *Time Blocks* to create the habits that lead to success.

Rejuvenating sleep is critical, because if you're exhausted, it's easy to lose control of your thoughts and emotions and begin to drift. *Time Blocking* for a good night sleep of six to eight hours is essential for maintaining *Sound Health*.

Utilizing *Spare Time* properly creates the *Success Mindset* of the *Pure Non-Drifter*. You will become excited about the time you have to achieve *Sound Health*. You will gain time to serve on boards, committees and other *Specialized Talent Teams* outside of work should you so desire. *Time Blocking* allows you to execute your *Faith-Based Actions* in a *Readiness Mindset*. This new version of you will create a level of confidence and harmony that you have never felt before.

Although it takes time to build *Time Blocking* routines, the result will replace pressure and anxiety with energy and harmony. You will be more efficient and effective in everything you do, and all your personal relationships will be strengthened.

The more productive you become through *Time Blocking* and *Controlled Attention*, the more others will seek your time. While you must be generous, you must guard your time.

If you easily say 'yes' to those in need of your talent and *Time* you may find yourself losing your *Time Blocking* discipline. You can avoid this by creating a *Time Block* dedicated to the role of community service. Then, without hesitation, you can say 'yes' to those seeking your time—if you so desire. Offer your *Time* during the *Time Blocks* that you've set aside for community service.

Remember, you're the one giving the gift of your *Time* and *Talent*—so respect your *Time* and keep your gift in its proper *Time Block*.

You also need to ask yourself—who warrants the gift of your *Time* and *Talent*?

If you are conditioned to serving others, to extremes, you will drain your resources. *Time* thieves will want to bring all their problems to you, suck all the energy out of you, and leave with their problems solved—and you with no energy left to achieve your goals, objectives, or *Life Purpose*.

Eliminate the *Time* thieves that aren't giving back, and then dedicate *Time* to those you love and those who deserve your *Time*. We are all unique. We should cherish our *Time* and *Talent* by protecting the way we utilize them.

Perhaps one of the most critical lessons to learn about guarding *Time* is to protect your transitions between *Time Blocks*.

When you're doing something that you love, it's easy to get caught up and lose track of *Time*. If you're not careful, you can let one *Time Block* run into the next one. This short-circuits your creativity and destroys your momentum. Work smart and end your *Time Blocks* as scheduled. You will return to that effort refreshed and with a higher level of creativity.

Ernest Hemingway used this technique to become a world-renowned novelist. He has been quoted as saying something like this:

"Always stop while things are going well—and don't think or worry about it until you start to write again. That way your subconscious will work on it while you rest."

Guarding your *Time Block* transitions also allows you to chain blocks of *Time* together, so that you build momentum in every area of your life.

In cryptocurrency, blockchains refer to a ledger of records, chained together in a way that solves the double-spending issue that many cryptocurrency systems used to face.

It can work the same in *Time Blocking*. As you chain your blocks of *Time* together, you can optimize your *Time*.

Block chaining your *Time* creates a sense of flow from one activity to the next. If you lack *Time* integrity, you're breaking the *Time Blocking Chain*. When you keep the flow, you develop routines and repetition that create the *Rhythm of Success* and ultimately the *Habit of Success*.

TAKEAWAYS

Eliminate the **Time thieves** that aren't giving back, and then dedicate *Time* to those you love and those who deserve your Time.

We should cherish our *Time* and *Talent* by protecting the way we utilize them.

It may take some time for people around you to adjust, and at first, you might experience a series of interruptions. Stick with block chaining your *Time* until others respect your *Time*.

In Life you are either in rhythm or out of rhythm.

When you are out of rhythm, how do you feel? Do you display a *Pleasing Personality*, or an unpleasant one? Do you live in a *Positive-State-of-Mind*, or a *Negative-State-of-Mind*?

Life is a series of rhythms. You choose what you think, therefore you choose the rhythms you are in.

Block chaining your *Time* reinforces the idea that you need to be present in the here and now, no matter what the activity is. When you're mentally present while relaxing, the rhythm of relaxation reenergizes you—when you are out of rhythm it drains you. When you're mentally present and enjoying your family, you are in the rhythm of relationships—when you're not mentally present you are out of rhythm, which triggers guilt and unhappiness that further drains you.

As you blockchain your *Time* to weave through all your life roles, and you are mentally present with a *Pleasing Personality*, people will gravitate to you rather than away from you.

Now let's discuss *Optimizing Money* to create your definition of *Rich*.

Think back to your earliest memory of money management, most likely given to you by your mom or dad. As children, most of us were taught that if we wanted something special, we needed to follow the work and save rule.

We found part-time jobs mowing lawns, weeding yards, shoveling snow, or babysitting. We worked, saved, counted, then worked,

Beyond Think and Grow Rich

saved, and counted some more. As our dollars and cents added up, we felt the joy of seeing our goal become crystal clear.

When we had saved enough money, the purchase day arrived. Our parents drove us to the store, and we made the purchase. And how sweet it was!

It was a double bonus. We experienced two joys: the joy of dreaming, saving, and celebrating as we earned, and the joy of finally making the purchase. This powerful lesson in delayed gratification taught us *Self-Discipline* and made us feel intelligent, capable, and self-reliant.

So, what happened to us? With such a powerful lesson learned, why did we change?

Eventually, as young earners we opened a bank account, and we were introduced to instant gratification—the debit card. From then on, our new best friend was constantly with us, in our pockets, wallets, and purses.

Debit cards gave us instant access to our bank accounts, whenever we wanted it. There was no need to write a check, enter it into a check register, and view our balance before we make a purchase.

Most people don't carry check registers anymore—and most people don't even have a savings account. The principle of saving ten percent of our earnings has gone out the window. Instead, we comingle all our money into one bank account and manage it with a debit card.

Every time we use our debit card, our account shows whether we still have money. We get that mental message, "You still have money, so keep spending," and we are enticed to spend until that balance is zero. We are conditioned to look at paydays as an automatic recharge of our debit cards, rather than as a day to pay bills, plan purchases, reconcile bank accounts, and set some money aside.

As a society, we have eliminated the habit of entering our purchases into a register and managing our balance—and we are paying the price for it.

TAKEAWAYS

As children, most of us were taught that if we wanted something special, we needed to follow the **work and save** rule.

> **This powerful lesson in delayed gratification taught us *Self-Discipline* and made us feel intelligent, capable, and self-reliant.**

Gaining the habit of using one of the many smartphone apps available to manage personal bank accounts is a significant step toward *Optimizing Money* and preventing or breaking the habit of living paycheck to paycheck.

In addition to gaining instant access to our bank account through a debit card, we were inundated with credit card offers. Introduction to the credit card taught us we could have whatever we wanted, whenever we want it. We could purchase big ticket items—many of them—with only one small monthly payment.

That is the trap. People who buy with credit are reduced to living outside of their means, until the debt payment becomes their ruler. Debt is their escort back to a *Negative-State-of-Mind* and the front door of the Negative Nuthouse, where they are welcomed by Dr. Doubt.

Getting out of debt—and staying out—may be the most crucial discipline of all. Debt causes you to lose money every day.

In a recent interview, Warren Buffet told the story of a woman who had $2,000. She asked him what her best investment would be. He asked if she had a credit card balance, and she said yes, thinking that everyone has a credit card balance. His next question was about the interest rate, which was 18 percent. His advice to her?

"Take your $2,000 and pay off your credit card."

Then, with humor, he said, "If you're willing to pay 18 percent, then I should give you, my money. There's no better investment than one that yields an 18% return. So why is it that you've given that income opportunity to your credit card company?"

Saving money is another essential *Live Ready*® discipline. Being frugal is vital to *Living Ready* and gaining financial freedom.

When my sons were preparing to leave the nest, I gave them a book and promised them if they read it and executed its principles, they would live a debt free life.

That book was *The Automatic Millionaire,* by David Bach. We discussed several of its money principles that are wise practices for anyone wishing to *Optimize Money*:

- **Continually save the first ten percent of your earnings.**
- **Invest to the maximum** in any 401K offered to you because most companies match your investment.
- **Buy a home and live in it until it's paid for.** Then, buy a second home and make your first home a rental property.
- **Make half your monthly house payment every two weeks.** This results in 13 monthly payments per year, rather than 12. With this strategy you trim years off your mortgage.
- **Eliminate expenses** that don't help you achieve your goals, objectives, or *Life Purpose*.
- **The latte rule**—If you buy a $5 latte every day, skip it and save the money. At the end of the month, you'll have around $150 to invest. With this saved money, pay one extra principal payment on your home mortgage.

I promised my sons if they followed *The Automatic Millionaire* principles, they would be millionaires by the time they were 45 years old.

Teaching our children solid financial principles allows them to develop a rhythm of wealth—so teach them well.

The rhythm of wealth is dependent on how you earn, save, spend, and invest your money. Most *Natural Drifters* fail to gain this rhythm.

TAKEAWAYS

Teaching our children **solid financial principles** allows them to develop a rhythm of wealth—so teach them well.

> **The rhythm of wealth is dependent on how you earn, save, spend, and invest your money.**

The *Destructive Drifter's* unpleasant personality makes it difficult for them to earn and save. Their instant gratification spending habits leave little to no excess money to invest. *Destructive Drifters* lack the discipline to master the *Optimizing Money* principle.

The *Pure Non-Drifters* embrace the *Optimizing Money* principle of forecasting and budgeting their *Money*. With *Accurate Thought,* they develop a clear *Creative Vision* and allocate their resources wisely. They understand and execute the earn, save, spend, and invest rule to achieve their goals, objectives, and *Life Purpose*.

Think back to Chapter Three, where we discussed *Specialized Talent Teams*. Learning the *Optimizing Money* principle follows the same process as developing a *Talent Team*.

At every income level, utilizing a percentage system can help you achieve your goals. The percentage amount will vary, depending on your personal circumstances, but you should always build your budget around a few critical categories.

In business, you need to budget expenses for insurance, overhead and salaries (including your own), taxes, marketing, investments, and savings.

When it comes to your personal income, consider the following five categories: insurance, living expenses, investment, charitable or religious contributions, and savings. Remember that the first and most important investment is to eliminate debt. Once you free yourself from the oppression of debt, you can save and invest in money-making opportunities.

If your income is not what you want it to be, you may not be able to plan for every category right away. Begin with what you have. Earn, save, spend, and invest wisely, and soon you will be able to plan for all five areas.

You must produce more than you consume. This requires the application of *Controlled Enthusiasm, Accurate Thought,* and *Self-Discipline.* You need all the *Readiness Mindset* principles to help you live within your means, stay out of debt, and save for the future.

In some cases, you will have to be more frugal than others. In every case, you will need to be wise in the way you spend. Make sure that your planned purchases are targeted toward your goals, objectives, or *Life Purpose.*

Don't wait so long to enjoy *Money* that you begin to feel deprived. Utilizing *Self-Discipline* to delay gratification is extremely important, but if you feel deprived for too long, you may slip into a *Negative-State-of-Mind* and make unplanned, unwise spending decisions to make yourself feel better. Retail therapy never works, because it derails your resources and distracts you from what you really want.

It is important to recognize that *Money* alone will not make you happy, but not having enough *Money* will prove to be very inconvenient.

Many people never really know what it means to live a *Rich* life. *Living Ready* starts by defining what *Rich* means to you. Take the five major roles in your life: family/friends, faith, community, health, and financial wealth. Think of these life roles as the combination to your *happiness consciousness* safe.

To gain access, create your combination settings, and develop a "*What is Rich*" statement for each of your life roles: family/friends, faith, community, health, and financial wealth.

Combining these five statements into one paragraph creates your personal definition of "*What is Rich*".

Just as you need to be mentally present in your *Time Blocks*, you need to be mentally present as you earn, save, spend, and invest your *Money*. Make sure you are spending at

TAKEAWAYS

Living Ready **starts by defining what** *Rich* **means to you. Take the five major roles in your life:** family/friends, faith, community, health, and financial wealth.

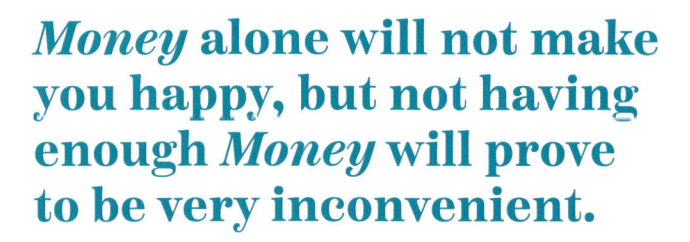

> ***Money* alone will not make you happy, but not having enough *Money* will prove to be very inconvenient.**

the right time, for the right reasons, in a timely manner that develops your rhythm of wealth.

Summary

As you develop your *Optimizing Time and Money* skillset, you'll likely go through an *Adversity Adjustment* that helps you better utilize both your *Time and Money*. This will enable you to take full of advantage of *Talent*, harmonious *Teamwork,* and other resources. You will *Live Ready*® and achieve riches in your family/friends, faith, community, health, and financial wealth life roles.

The Optimizing Time and Money *challenge*

Access QR code
or at eleadertech.com/OTMC

Beyond Think and Grow Rich

"We are what we repeatedly do. Excellence, then, is not an act, but a habit."

— ARISTOTLE

CHAPTER TEN

The Promise

GOOD OR BAD, YOU WILL RECEIVE THE *REWARDS* OR *Penalties* of your thoughts and actions. This is the *Promise* of the *Law of Habits*. This simple truth is the basis for *Living Ready*.

Living Ready begins when you take charge of your thoughts and actions. Whenever they are repeated intensely and frequently, Nature promises they'll become a habit and you will get back whatever you put forth.

We are ruled by our habits. The purpose of this entire book is to help you replace bad habits and their *Penalties* with good habits and their *Rewards*.

Your thoughts and actions develop your habits, then your habits develop who you are.

The *Promise* of the *Law of Habits* is backed by Nature. In the natural world, we see repeating patterns on every level: the solar system mimics the atom, and the spiral shape found in galaxies is reflected in snail shells. Even the Golden Ratio is found in both architecture and the symmetry of human faces. They are *Universal* and unchangeable. Patterns develop habits. When you develop positive patterns, they will develop the *Habit of Success* within you.

The *Law of Habits* is neutral, just like your subconscious—the 80% of your mind that we studied in the *Brain Model*. It will accept and execute any pattern, positive or negative. You develop your habits when you choose or accept your thoughts and actions.

Seeding your mind with ideas for success and happiness can only be achieved while in a *Positive-State-of-Mind*. To create good habits that help you get what you want in life, it is essential to maintain a *Positive Mindset*—otherwise, you'll create negative bad habits. One bad habit often overshadows dozens of good habits.

In earlier chapters, you were introduced to the three phases of the journey to success. You start by accepting the challenge of *Controlled Success*, to develop the *Rhythm of Success*, to achieve the *Habit of Success*. This is a *Universal* pattern—it is the *Law of Habits*, proving you can *Stop Drifting*® and permanently alter your life setting from negative to positive.

If your life is not what you want it to be, it is directly connected to your habits. If you take charge of your habits, anything is possible.

Even now, I marvel at how the *Promise* of the *Law of Habits* impacted me. As a young boy raised in foster care, I stumbled to find my way. It took me some time to realize I could not do this alone. I was pointed in the right direction first by my fifth-grade teacher, Sam Francis, and later, by Robert E. Farrell. They taught me the power of *thought*, *purpose*, and *action* to participate in the game of life and, more importantly, how to win it.

Changing my habits enabled me to utilize all the *Live Ready*® principles. As a result, I moved from a negative thought setting to a positive one and achieved the *Habit of Success*. My life changed, and I experienced achievements beyond my wildest dreams.

The *Promise* of the *Law of Habits* is demonstrated just as beautifully in the lives of every successful person I have ever met.

Remember the David Durocher story. When he was apprehended for dealing drugs and was facing a long prison sentence, he realized, for the first time in his life, what his destructive life patterns and habits had produced. At that time, he did

TAKEAWAYS

Good or bad, you will receive the **Rewards or Penalties** of your thoughts and actions. This is the **Promise** of the **Law of Habits**.

> **Your thoughts and actions develop your habits, then your habits develop who you are.**

not know how, but he knew he had to change or die in prison.

This enabled him to seek the opportunity to attend Delancey Street, where he was introduced to *Controlled Success*. This later created his *Rhythm of Success,* and after hundreds and hundreds of days, developed into his *Habit of Success*. Because he changed his thought setting from negative to positive, he was able to change his life. David spent the first half of his life destroying the lives of others. Today, David is enjoying the second half of his life saving the lives of others.

Jeff Bezos utilized the *Promise* of the *Law of Habits* to become one of the richest people in the world, rising from his humble beginning to create Amazon.com and Blue Origin. He developed a positive mindset and focused his thoughts and actions with intensity on achieving both his *Business* and *Life Purpose*. He changed the way merchandise is sold and purchased worldwide and built a rocket ship to successfully achieve space travel.

It was the same with Britnie Turner. Her first goal in life was to become a missionary, and at that time she disliked the thought of the corporate business world. Once she realized that God was directing her toward entering the business world, she altered her thinking and actions. She studied real estate and the lives of successful people, learned how to create *Specialized Talent Teams*, and built habits that sustained both her personal growth and the growth of her business empire. She is now utilizing the *Promise* of the *Law of Habits* to significantly improve people's lives all around the world.

Misty Copeland used the *Promise* of *Law of Habits* to overcome her poverty-stricken beginning in life. As she focused her thoughts on her love of dance, she developed *Faith-Based Action* habits. She gained *Self-Discipline* and built a solid framework of daily practice.

Her hard work paid off. She achieved her goal of becoming a Principal Dancer with the American Ballet Theater, authored several books, and is now using the *Promise* of the *Law of Habits* to help children of every color thrive through ballet.

John Sachtouros, known as 'the man who never gives up and always keeps moving forward,' utilized the *Promise* of the *Law of Habits* to become a millionaire. He is now headed toward his new *Life Purpose* of helping "Beyond a Billion" people to achieve their purpose.

Although John started life out in the United States of America as an immigrant worker waiting tables in an Italian restaurant, his *Positive-State-of-Mind* and drive enabled him to discover his *Life Purpose*. He built his thoughts, actions, and habits to achieve a *Readiness Mindset*. As he developed the *Habit of Success*, he built his network marketing empire from the ground up. He validates the *Promise* of the *Law of Habits* with his success of providing worldwide learning opportunities through his newest company, ASCIRA.

Truett Cathy's belief in the *Promise* of the *Law of Habits* enabled him to grow the Chick-Fil-A business. His thoughts and habits built his company around the principle of a *Pleasing Personality*, which became the key ingredient in Chick-Fil-A's success.

Jim Stovall utilized the *Promise* of the *Law of Habits* to overcome a devastating life challenge. When he was diagnosed with macular degeneration, he made the necessary *Adversity Adjustment* in his thoughts, actions, and habits. He started the Narrative Television Network for the blind, became a millionaire and a philanthropist, and authored several books. As a public speaker, he now teaches others how to find the seed of the greater benefit in their challenges, so they, too, can utilize the *Promise* of the *Law of Habits* to achieve what they want in life.

Dr. José Antonio Calzada used the *Promise* of the *Law of Habits* to become one of the most renowned physicians for health and longevity care in the world. His habits began as a young boy, when he studied plants and herbs to learn how to heal

TAKEAWAYS

These powerful *Live Ready*® principles will not become a habit until they are used in your daily life, and you teach them to others.

> **I encourage you to join me in the service of others through 'Time Tithing'.**

others. As a young man his thoughts, actions, and habits impacted his choices, which kept him on the path of becoming a doctor and true healer. Now he teaches his patients how to create and maintain health by staying in a *Positive-State-of-Mind* and practicing *Sound Health* principles.

This pattern of excellence is repeated in the lives of successful people everywhere.

I promised Mr. Farrell that I would repay him for the gift of knowledge and time he gave me by coaching and mentoring others who would surely drift into my life in search of direction and purpose. I encourage you to join me in the service of others through 'Time Tithing'.

These powerful *Live Ready*® principles will not become a habit until they are used in your daily life, and you teach them to others. When you do, you unleash the power of the *Law of Habits* in your own life and in the lives of the people you serve. That is the *Promise*. It works automatically, and it never fails.

It's also my promise to you. Take the journey. *Live Ready*®. If I can do it, you can do it, too.

Live Ready® Deep Dive Discussion
with David R. Ibarra:

Access QR code or at eleadertech.com/LRDD

Beyond Think and Grow Rich

IN GRATITUDE & ACKNOWLEDGEMENT

To Don Green, Executive Director of The Napoleon Hill Foundation, and Lionel Sosa, author of *Think and Grow Rich – a Latino Choice*—for being my sounding boards as I wrote this book.

I want to acknowledge the impact Dr. Napoleon Hill made on my life and my career. His book, *Think and Grow Rich*, was the starting point of my success and the inspiration for this book.

To Dr. James Hill, the grandson of Dr. Napoleon Hill, for sharing his Reticular Activating System – RAS research with me, which I used in this book.

To Dave Durocher, Britnie Turner, Dr. John Sachtouras, and Dr. José Antonio Calzada for granting me interviews so their stories could be included in this book.

To S. Truett Cathy, Jeff Bezos, Misty Copeland and Jim Stovall for the inspiration I received from each of their lives.

To Gwen Bristol, Wade Taylor, and Colby Hill for proofing my work and providing suggestions for ways to improve the flow of the story.

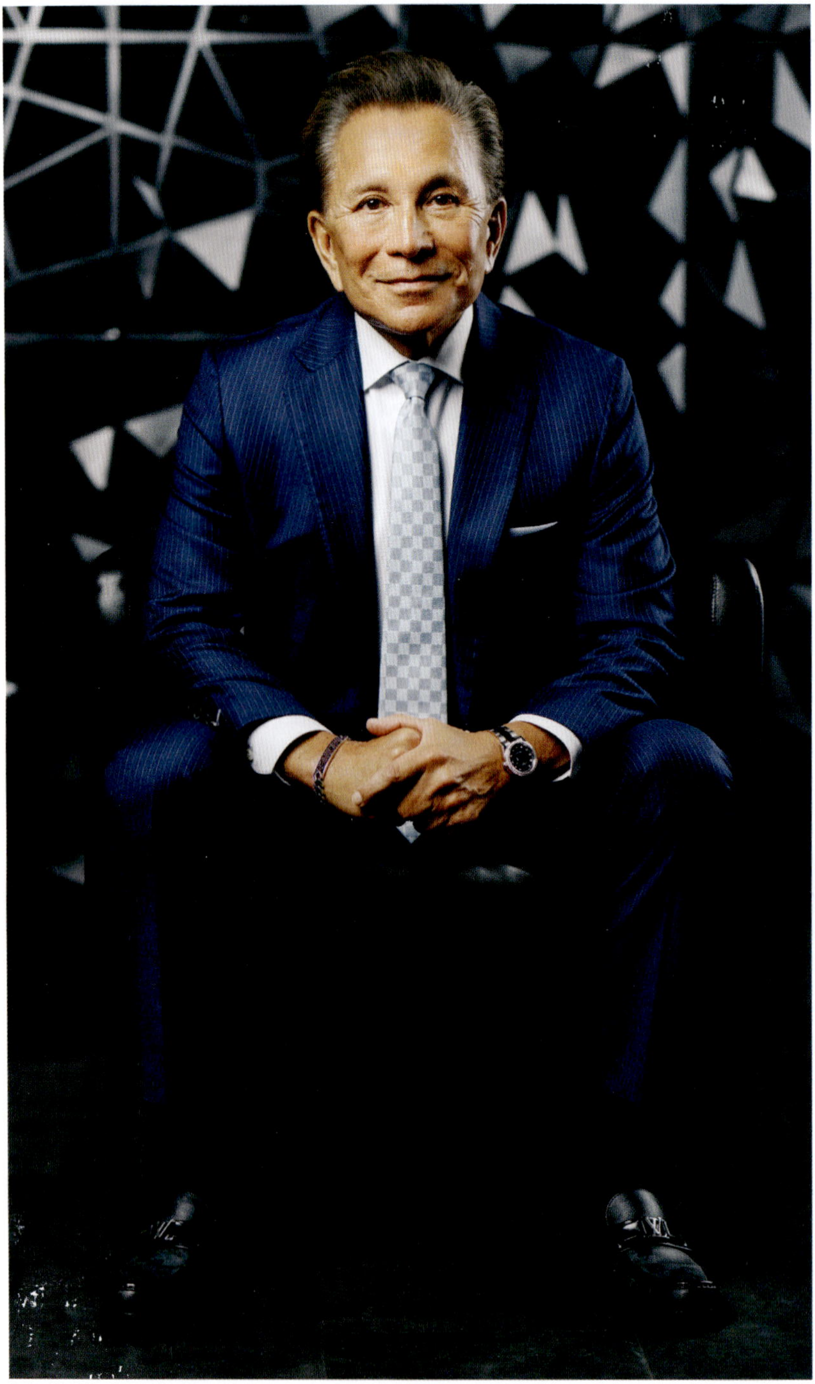

"Whether you think you can, or you think you can't—you're right."

— HENRY FORD

David R. Ibarra
AUTHOR | SPEAKER | ENTREPRENEUR | COMMUNITY LEADER

If you want to inspire people to believe success was meant for them, hire David to help get it done.

"I've had the good fortune to attend several of David Ibarra's keynote presentations in New York City, Detroit, and Chengdu China. His enthusiasm is infectious, his ability to educate is impressive, and his dedication to success is inspirational."

— **CHARLIE VOGELHEIM,** HOST OF MOTOR TREND AUDIO, PAST EXECUTIVE EDITOR AT KELLEY BLUE BOOK AND VICE PRESIDENT AT J.D. POWER AND ASSOCIATES

To learn more about Living Ready on Your Journey to Success, and to hire or schedule a visit DavidRI...